ADVANCE PRAISE

"It's the journey, not the destination" is now a common refrain. But in reading the testimonies in A Seat at The Table, I am convinced that destinations matter. Destinations are places of rest, reflection, and even redemption. When they don't exist, you hope someone is trying to build them. That is just what Pastor Dawn and her community did at The Table. The people of God found not only refuge there, but they were also equipped to be sent forth for their vital work in the world. What a marvelous portrait of what the Church can be!"

Chris Sanders, MDiv
Executive Director, Tennessee Equality Project
and Tennessee Equality Project Foundation

"Stories move in circles, they do not move in straight lines. There are stories inside of stories and stories between stories. A Seat at The Table provides a pathway for discovery that finding your way through them is as easy as it is hard to find your way home when you are lost. This book invites readers to not only look around but to listen. Reminding us that our collective humanity is bound up together."

Tonya Bramlage, DVM, PC
Mastermarks Ministries, FL

"The collected theological depth in these personal stories is profoundly moving. In a world desperate for hope, this book illustrates how compassionate interconnection builds and transforms communities. An inspiring read."

Suzanne DeWitt Hall (Zan)
Author of The Language of Bodies *and* Where True Love Is Devotionals

"Whether you're religious or agnostic, this beautifully raw collection of stories has something to resonate with every heart."

Megan Grisolano, Producer Nashville PBS

"Each of us lives our lives through the lens of our own experience. As pastors, we become a part of the lives of the people in our congregations. Pastors don't often ask how we impact the lives of those in the pews, but Rev. Dawn took a traumatic event, the unexpected closure of The Table, to ask the people—how was your life changed by The Table? Rev. Dawn ministered to the people on the margins and we get to read the stories of how the ministry Rev. Dawn created at The Table changed their lives. Each story, including Rev. Dawn's narrative, is powerful, vulnerable, and the truth."

The Reverend Sister Nicole Garcia
Pastor, Epiphany Lutheran Church, Denver
Novice, Order of Lutheran Franciscans

"The Table wasn't built with grand cathedrals or endless committees. It was built with open hands, open hearts, and a fierce, unshakable belief that everyone deserves a seat at God's table. The Table was sacred — something the world desperately needed but didn't yet know how to ask for. These were not typical church services. They were sanctuaries within a sanctuary—safe, sacred spaces where healing could begin. I knew, even before we gathered for the first time, that The Table would be holy ground, creating space for countless people to come back to God after years of exile."

Olivia Hill, Speaker
Metro Nashville Council at-Large

"One of Steven Covey's seven habits for effectiveness states, 'Seek first to understand and then to be understood.' Another wise adage says, 'People will forget what you say, but they will always remember how you made them feel.' With this wisdom in mind, even pastors most stringently opposed to normalizing LGBTQ+ relationships can gain understanding from this collection of stories because they inform how those testifying felt at church, even in many matters not related to sexuality. For thousands of years people have gathered around the fire to tell stories because stories connect us. These stories transcend LGBTQ+ issues because they describe the yearnings for connection we all have."

Brad Bull, PhD, MDiv, LMFT
Nashville, TN

"A Seat at The Table is a beautiful testament to the power of faith, healing, and community. These stories shine a light on the resilience of the LGBTQ+ community and the sacred spaces where all are welcome. As the founder of Free Mom Hugs, I know the life-changing impact of being seen, heard, and loved and this book is full of those moments."

Sara Cunningham
Founder, Free Mom Hugs

"Pastor Dawn provides us with a passionate, authentic chorus of voices. These stories of faith speak truth and power to the everyday reality faced by many members of the Body of Christ in our world today. Listen, learn, and hear how God is calling you at work in our neighbors. Their witness matters."

Rev. Alex Smith, ELCA

"True to form, Pastor Dawn didn't write a book about The Table. Instead, she offers The Table. Pull up a chair. Experience it for yourself. In this way, the ministry lives on…"

Kent Wilson
former ELCA Pastor and
Founder, Find Your Way Forward

"One of my favorite hymns is 'For Everyone Born.' The first verse starts 'For everyone born, a place at the table.' At The Table there was truly a place for everyone, especially those excluded or wounded at other churchy tables. But belonging is only the beginning. The beloveds who share their stories within these pages remind us that when people find their place, they also discover their voice, their gifts, and their passions. They learn to reframe, reform, and reset the other tables in their lives. They become 'creators of justice and joy' wherever they go, and God delights in them, just as God always has. May it be so for us as well."

The Reverend Kari Niedermaier
All Saints Lutheran Church, Port Orange, FL
Just Love Co-Chair, Florida Bahamas Synod, ELCA

"I appreciate Rev. Bennett's A Seat at The Table because it resonates deeply with my own experience: that healthy, functioning communities are often not permanent, but experimental. Their depth and uniqueness can be so subversive that some people can't even recognize their legitimacy — and, at times, powerful forces rise up to resist them, making their continuation unsustainable. I often wonder if this kind of temporary, almost guerrilla-style community is the only way such spaces can exist, not just because they resist institutionalization, but because they boldly declare they don't need it. That's why, when someone asks if I know of a good church community, I'll often respond, 'This one, for now, while it is still around, is trying to be.'"

David Hayward
aka NakedPastor

"A Seat at The Table gives voice and power to those who so often are silenced in today's churches. One of the many things I have learned since the death of my son is the importance of sharing our stories to help make change. Thanks to these powerful stories told through strong courageous voices we can see that we do not need to simply continue to foolishly conform to the status quo or patterns of our harmful past teachings and dogma that has caused so much pain to so many in the LGBTQ+ community and other marginalized groups. But rather we can transform our minds, faith, and teachings to help foster hope, healing, and life for all God's children. Helping all to know God's good, pleasing and perfect will as beautiful children of God, created in God's image and surrounded by God's unconditional love.

We need more faith communities like The Table to build people up, heal the traumatized and show abundant unconditional love and grace to everyone, especially the LGBTQ+ community. May A Seat at The Table continue the good work and ministry started at The Table by Pastor Dawn and may it be a blessing to many."

Jane Clementi (she/her/hers)
Co-Founder and CEO of Tyler Clementi Foundation

A SEAT AT THE TABLE
STORIES OF FAITH, HEALING, AND REBIRTH

REV. DAWN BENNETT

Copyright © 2025 by Rev. Dawn Bennett

All rights reserved.

No part of this book may be reproduced in any form or by any electronic or mechanical means, including information storage and retrieval systems, without written permission from the author, except for the use of brief quotations in a book review.

Tehom Center Publishing is a 501(c)3 nonprofit publishing feminist and queer authors, with a commitment to elevate BIPOC writers. Its face and voice is Rev. Dr. Angela Yarber.

Paperback ISBN: 978-1-966655-62-6

Ebook ISBN: 978-1-966655-63-3

CONTENTS

Acknowledgments   13
Foreword   15

Part I
LOOKING INWARD

Reasons and Seasons   21
Lexi's Life Shift   29
Heather's Healing Journey   45
Charis: Two PK's in a Pod   59

Part II
LOOKING OUTWARD

Jessica's New Name   79
Christopher's Imagination   97
The Intern Now Reverend Wesley King   115
Lance's Search for Welcome   133

Part III
MAKING HISTORY

Olivia's Legacy   139
Ginger Widens WELCA   147
Veronika's New Stage   163

Part IV
COMMUNITY CONNECTIONS

Music City Sisters of Perpetual Indulgence   189
TDOR, IDOA, Transletes, and Prom   191
LifeNotes & Wondering Questions   195
At The Table God's Beloved Sheet Music   199

PART V
THE MAKING AND BREAKING OF A PASTOR   201

This gift is dedicated to every person and community partner whose voice has been lifted from the ashes of church-based trauma, political discrimination and family rejection.
You are seen here. You are affirmed here. Your life is sacred space.

And to KLH, who while grown, still allow me to be their Mom.

In loving memory of
Phillip Michael Thomas, a Nashville ground rod,
fierce LGBQ+ sibling, and Trans Community ally.
May you rest in peace our dear brother in Christ.

ACKNOWLEDGMENTS

There is likely no way to capture every name I owe thanks to. Mission Development (aka church planting) is a process always on the move. Its purpose is growth in as many directions as possible. I was blessed to be the person in charge of the growth of this church. Over the years I partnered with community organizers, non and for profit organizations, other clergy (irrespective of faith, denomination or religion), interviewers and media producers too numerous to count, and individuals who were curious and angry enough to ask holy questions. These are the real nuts and bolts of who and what The Table grew to be. To that end, while I opened my arms as wide as possible, I limited the printed names to those who were active members and community partners at the time of our closing.

Acknowledgements & Thank yous: Greg B, Dawn L, Adam S, Matthew M, Shannon M, Tiffany K, Amy L, Molly B, John S, Devin R, Frank M, Georgia M, Steven R, Lexi S, Olivia H, Wesley K, Heather W, Charis A, Ginger C, Jessica L, Music City Sisters of Perpetual Indulgence, Nashville Pride, Nashville PFLAG, Mac H, Tina T, Kathy H, Phil Michael T, Travis M, Jeff B, Kevin S, Melissa F-S, Devin S, Travis W, David & Cathryne H, Rick R, Trevor K, Grace B, Allison E, Angela P, Steve & Billy, Nancy K, Rj R, Marcy N, Dahron J, Christopher F, Tank M, Glen A, Steph B, Kent W, Declan & Zan. If I left out your name please know we hold you dear in our hearts!

Special acknowledgements are given to Bishop Emeritus, The Reverend Dr. H. Julian Gordy, who while I was still in seminary, believed in me and my audacity to build such a ministry. Without it, neither the vision nor this book would have ever come to life; Also The Reverend Dr. John Swyers who has, from the moment we met, reminded me daily what a beautiful, holy mess I am. I realize keeping me "in the ring" is a full-time job, for which I pray God blesses you richly.

Julian and John, *I thank my God in all my remembrance of you.* (Philippians 1:3)

FOREWORD

*God has shown you, O mortal, what is good.
And what does the Lord require of you?
To act justly and to love mercy
and to walk humbly with your God.*

— MICAH 6:8

Prophetic voices do not just come via fire upon the altar that consumes the sacrifice, and then licks up the water around. People, pastors, and churches, are often a prophetic witness to the call and response to God—a call and response that rarely happens in the comfortable, and where the current order fits the notions we have been taught. The rub is that prophetic witness lives in the uncomfortable tension of what is and what God wants to see.

The Table, and their pastor—Dawn Bennett, were people willing to live in the tension of what *is*, as they worked toward the Kingdom that is becoming. Their joyous "yes" to so much brought healing to many. Their faithful presence allowed many

FOREWORD

to know that they were created as unique and wonderful image bearers of God. Their generosity of grace, undeserved favor, opened heart-doors that had been slammed shut for years (most often deservedly so). Their magnanimity of mercy allowed them to touch a world that is often cruel and unkind. And, lest I forget, their actions that worked to ensure people were treated justly, is a prophetic witness to who God is calling us to be as a people.

These stories and interviews are really stories of death and resurrection. The cycle that seems to never end for those who believe beyond themselves; Who believe in something, someone, some cause— that transforms the person into the shining radiance they are. The stories are not all happy-happy, joy-joy. I am convinced that these recollections will speak hope to someone who reads them, because we all long to know we are not alone in this world (and the next). Hope is the beginning of every resurrection story, and finding our tribe—as The Table did—allowed many to find *their* tribe. As you read these stories, my prayer is that you find yourself in one, or many.

As I wind up, I want to share a specific word about Reverend Dawn Bennett. I believe with my entire being that God made her for such a time as this. A woman after God's own heart, seeing people as fully as anyone can, and loving them as they were and into who they are becoming. The task of a church planter (non ELCA language) is never easy, and they have to be willing to roll with the punches: Shifting paradigms from preCOVID to after, to the changing nature of the ministry of The Table, due to the needs and saints presented by God for ministry—made it dynamic and growing.

Her voice of compassion and recasting vision for the faith aided many. Her voice is/was prophetic as were the people who were part of The Table. Her story is the story of "even if," the story of a faith that dies and rises again.

That is the real story of faith: doing the next right thing, even if the cost is high. Her core character, love, and desire for mercy were always evident and understated. It was never about her, but about the people she was called to serve. May she keep that voice in all she does until she is called to her eternal home.

Reverend Greg Bullard, Pastor
Covenant of the Cross, Madison, TN

PART I
LOOKING INWARD

Reasons and Seasons: An Author's Note
Lexi's Life Shift
Heather's Healing Journey
Charis: Two PKs in a Pod

REASONS AND SEASONS

AN AUTHOR'S NOTE

Every new beginning comes from another beginning's end.

— SENECA

October 13, 2024 was the last time we held worship at The Table. My only regret looking back on that particular night, is that it was the one service we did not stream live and likely should have. At least as they are compiled here, the words so heavy, yet so holy, will have a chance to live on in the spirits of those gathered within their pages. There are some helpful tidbits to share, here in the beginning, that will serve as the pilot to the most endearing flight of holy hospitality that could come of such a gathering. I will begin by sharing the main excerpts from my final sermon in that blessed pulpit that gave so much back to us. Followed by details of clarity that will lay the foundation of the stories you will later read.

In 2019, when I began praying about how to build this church, I distinctly remember talking to God and saying, "I don't know what they need." God answered, "Ask them." I said, "I'm not sure how to help them." Again, God whispered to me, "Ask them."

So, from day one—THAT was the humble beginnings of ministry and outreach here at The Table. Two simple questions. And only two. It's all I have ever asked myself, each of you, and every community member we have served: what do you need? and how can I help? Two invitations, rooted in unconditional love and curiosity have carried us to this day.

Putting together something to say for today was very difficult. Excruciating in fact. I sat mostly in silence this week as I tended to the tasks I was given, preparing to close our doors forever. Prayer and discernment about what to preach came and went in tandem with my gut wrenching sobs and enormous gratitudes too numerous to count.

I am so grateful for every person who walked through our doors and sat in the seats we offered whether in worship Sunday nights, or community outreach during the months. Every person is sacred. Every story is holy. And every encounter was an appointment with the Divine. At least that's how I see it—how I've always seen it.

Throughout many of his letters, the apostle Paul says some version of, 'I thank God for all my remembrance of you. I pray for you daily and lift you up with prayers of mercy, peace and liberation.' I too lift you in prayer daily. I too thank God for you, Beloveds. I thank God for the ways you have taught me how to be a pastor. I thank God for the ways you have taught me how to be a fighter and a warrior; and a public voice for marginalized people groups. I thank God for the ways you have allowed me to creatively explore what God could mean by 'unconditional love' and 'radical faith.' I thank God for who we became over the years: a little band of prophetic misfits.

A few years ago, you gave me the opportunity to introduce you to a new way of thinking, which for many of you, flies in the face of what you previously learned about religion, faith, Christianity, church life, love, God's grace, and the list goes on...

You allowed me to introduce you to a teaching method I developed called the 3 R's. We talked about it weekly, "Reframe. Reform. Reclaim." We didn't shy away from hard scriptures in this place. We didn't lean out. Instead, we deliberately leaned in. We stayed. We remained—until we found life-giving messages in this Breath of God called the Bible. This book has been used to harm a great number of people, ourselves included. And I hope, over the years, I have given you a new way forward that you can practice in your daily life; And that this book has an opportunity to be used to bring great healing to you and those you choose to share it with!

Each week we reframed by leaning in until we saw ourselves located and represented in the text. And when we found ourselves and our lived experiences represented, we began to poke and prod and dream and explore and question and doubt and seek—until we are able to re-form new narratives: Narratives that are life-giving and empowering. Narratives that promote health and wellness and healing. New narratives that restore our faith and push us beyond our comfort zone. Narratives that spur us on to take action, until FINALLY, we stand on our own two feet and reclaim our faith. You've done some good, hard, spiritual work, Beloveds.

It's been a tough week…and this is a tough night. But this is not the end of our story. I AM SO, SO PROUD OF YOU! It is not lost on me, just as it is not lost on any of you, that most of the people in this room, and thousands of others who were served through us over the years, have experienced religious harm and trauma from people like me standing in a pulpit just like this. So, I want to affirm you and commend you in your bravery and courage; and for taking a chance that 'it just might be different this time.' And it was. And it is. Beloveds, we have built something beautiful here.

We can find comfort and strength in Paul's Benediction to the church in Thessalonica, as we are the new generation. So well done, good and faithful servants. Well done, for doing the hard things. Well done, for loving yourself enough to stand up and be counted—instead of sit down and be silenced. Well done, that you have come to this place in your faith journey with these new set of options.

Now, we have new seeds to plant! Seeds that will undoubtedly grow a new harvest—full of new fruits! God's Word does not come back void, Beloveds. Trust that—even when you can't see it. We all have an opportunity to take what we have learned and experienced here and plant it in God's garden all around, wherever we have a plot to call our own.

Over the coming weeks we will each continue to process our grief and sorrow. I encourage you Friends, for every grief, raise up a gratitude. And for every sorrow plant a new seed. From day one I have preached the same line of scripture to you all, Jeremiah 1:5: The Lord said, "I knew you before I formed you in the womb." Beloveds, God did not bring you this far! or me! or The Table! to dump us off and have us be done. Many of you waited a mighty long time to see in yourself what God sees in you. It's been a mighty long time and a lot of work for some of you to agree with God, that you ARE sacred and holy! Do you really think God's gonna let that be the end? Think again, Friends.

God continued to breathe life into Jeremiah's ministry despite the struggle and chaos that swirled around him. In Chapter 29 verse 11, God shored-up Jeremiah's faith—empowered him to go and share God's unconditional love with everyone he could despite any blowback or speed bumps. God told Jeremiah, "I have a plan and a purpose for your life. They are plans for good and not for disaster, to give you a future and a hope." Jeremiah was a prophet of OLD. And we, dear church, are prophets of this New Age. May it be so. Amen.

Damn. It still hurts. Rereading it is empowering though. When I began praying about this book and how to begin, most everything came flooding back in. And this time, with a renewed sense of purpose. Yes, there was more but what you just read was the seedling for what you are about to read. We were charged with planting new seeds, in new soil. We were charged with tending our hearts and each other in love and kindness. We did that. We continue to do that. This project is evidence of the truth that God's Word does not come back void.

The culminating purpose of this writing project puts to holy use the healing we received through our association with The Table and choosing to leave that healing in a public space, as evidence to hopefully help somebody else heal. To that end, there was only one right way to write this book. It had to be in keeping with our Mission & Vision Statement and pay homage to our Welcome Statement:

Mission Statement: The Table promotes spiritual well being for LGBTQIA+ and minority people groups in the exploration of self, faith, community and the deeper issues of being and belonging.

Vision Statement: The Table centers the voices of LGBTQIA+ people and vulnerable identities as we form intentional faith communities and opportunities for engagement that are inclusive of all and alienating of none.

Welcome Statement: The Table is a LGBTQIA+ centered faith collective committed to the work of social justice and racial equity. We welcome those who are seeking God's love and grace as a first timer or a lifer. Everyone has a seat at our table and we affirm people of all races, ethnicities, cultures, abilities, age, sexual orientations, gender identities, gender expressions, and relationship status. We strive for whole-person wellness without regard to addictions, physical or mental health, imprisonment, socio-economic status, or that which divides. We actively seek unity. (Also noteworthy, we read this aloud together at the start of every worship service.)

The ministry is closed now and we never did get a specific reason as to why, making it unanticipated, unexpected, and a traumatic shock to our systems. What little I was told about, I am not at liberty to discuss. The closure left a great deal of spiritual damage in its wake, caused by the Synod and Institutional Church. Nonetheless, we are all better for its existence. All of us, including the Synod and the Institution. The members are better; the Church is better, our city, state and country are all better. And most importantly, God was glorified in the process.

I would be remiss if I did not lift up the scores of ministry colleagues who have stood by me every step of the journey as I built and pastored this church. Some still stand by me today. I will forever be indebted to the ELCA Lutheran and ecumenical colleagues in Nashville, TN who watched from the sidelines, cried, prayed, advocated, and provided direct support to us. Your labor was not in vain and your friendship will forever be a gratitude I hold dear.

As for the guest writers who joined me here, I learned so much in these interviews, information I did not know before. How I could pastor somebody for five years and learn such new things—it has really been a very joyous experience for me. Painful sometimes because the pain we have talked about is real pain. We did not hold back. Like I told one person whose story reveals more pain than potentially any of us: this is your story, this is your truth. This is not a feel-good book, it is a true 'experience of transformation' project. The reason our stories are important is because The Table mattered. It lifted up people's lives in real time.

I am educated and certified in religious trauma syndrome & recovery practices. As such, I am a trauma-informed[1] pastor and chaplain— important to mention because while each story is told in the words of my guests, not all of the language used is in keeping with how I identify with the Holy—or how you may

---

1. The key principles of Trauma-informed Pastoral Care (TiPC) prioritize physical, emotional and spiritual safety built on trustworthiness and transparency. Other elements foster collaboration and choice, and recognizing the influence of cultural, historical, and gender factors in experiences of trauma and healing. More information is available via internet search.

identify. I extend my sincere gratitude to Tehom Center Publishing for their allowance of gendered language for "God" as it pushes against their guidelines.

Biblical translation has historically been done by [white] men and therefore the male gendering of "God" has been etched in our minds for millennia. We must understand this is a political move, not a God-ordained one. Early translators have done their apostolic duty by keeping the story alive through the ages; however, it came at a grave cost to faithful followers. So now, the healing work from religious trauma is invasive and eternal, always seeking out ways to untangle the mess humanity has made as we ardently work to understand and share the message and ministry of Jesus. This work will never end. And never should, lest the Christian life be in vain.

As you embark on each chapter dear reader, know that you are on sacred ground. Even throughout our stories we wrestled to find ourselves located in sacred texts, then worked to reframe, reform and reclaim our faith. My hope is that readers find themselves in the stories in a way that helps them heal and reclaim theirs too. There is healing in the heartbreak and in the heartwork. We trust God will take our collective stories and enliven them to help others. The church may be closed but the work will always continue. I'll end this introduction with the way I began weekly worship:

Imagine us sitting together in a group. I walk out to the center with my Tibetan bowl nestled in one hand and a wooden mallet in the other. I gently invite you to center yourself, close your eyes and take a few deep breaths. With each strike of my mallet, the bowl resonates into the spiritual abyss, until finally, we are in silence together. Just long enough to embrace that holy moment.

God be with you, Beloveds.
Rev. Dawn Bennett

LEXI'S LIFE SHIFT

"...a lot of that has come from my time at The Table and being able to grow into a person who knows their worth instead of their worth being based on everybody else's opinion or needs."

PASTOR'S PERSPECTIVE

Lexi served as Chairperson of the Advisory Team at The Table. That didn't come up much in our conversation but as I look back on her position on the Advisory Board, Lexi provided a stable rudder from which I was able to lead us in a solid and noteworthy direction. I am thankful she followed me around and kept me on track. It was a wild ride at times and I am grateful.

A big part of Mission Development in church building involves growing and stretching. Over the years, I watched Lexi grow and stretch in her personal life and in her church membership. We moved worship spaces four times. We began in a classroom upstairs, moved to the basement, renovated a children's chapel and finally took our final space in a bonafide chapel. Like the movement of our sacred worship spaces, watching Lexi move and rehab the spaces in her life was equally sacred.

How did you find The Table and how did you find Pastor Dawn?

I found The Table through an online search. I googled LGBT-friendly churches in Nashville and The Table popped up. So I decided I would try it. I had no idea who you were until I walked in the door. The church I was going to was an affirming church but there was a shift in leadership. The priest left and I was finding myself responsible for more and more things that I did not want to be responsible for. I was no longer being fed by the church I was going to, so I was looking for somewhere to be fed.

The Table was never supposed to be a permanent situation for me. It was supposed to be *'this is how I'm getting [spiritually] fed while I'm figuring out all this other stuff at this other church.'* I never got back to a place where I felt comfortable in my former church, so I left them permanently after about six months. Then, I became a full-time member of The Table.

It was September 2021, the world had just begun opening up from COVID. We were already streaming services. As I walked in, you were running around like a chicken with your head cut off, trying to get the technology to work. I laughed and thought, *what is going on*?! G was there and introduced herself to me. She seemed to be the calm in the storm at that point. I looked around and thought, *okay, they're friendly*. Even in the early years there was a lot going on. We moved the worship space around and each time we inched closer to what became our final resting place in the Open Seating Chapel.

What was the condition of your faith prior to joining The Table?

I've always been a self proclaimed church nerd. I have some very good friends who are pastors who definitely affirm that in me, that I am a church nerd. But I was fried from being at the other church. I had nothing left to give because they just kept taking and not refilling my cup in any way, shape, or form. That was why I was even looking for a filler church to begin with. I had nothing left to give, of any of me at that point, because of my home situation, my church situation, and a million other things.

I've always been a giver and a carer, not a taker. But I had reached the point where I knew I needed to start taking some stuff for me, or I was going to lose everything. I knew if that happened, I would not be able to function in any form of caretaking which is very important to me. So my faith was stable, it just needed to be relocated.

[I asked Lexi how it was that her faith was stable. I invited her to share early life experiences because, for many of us in the queer community, it is those early life experiences, when intertwined with religious experience, that often make us and/or break us as we grow into adulthood. Lexi, like several of the others as you will read, was gracious enough to share.]

Every time something bad happened from the time I was sixteen when my Dad died, it was a turn *to* Jesus not a turn *from* Jesus. He [Jesus] has always been my center and my source of comfort. I have never questioned His being there or being a part of my life. Now, my younger brother is the exact opposite. When our Dad died, he turned *from* Jesus and is still mad at God for taking our Dad when He did. My brother still feels like he got cheated out of having a father. Whereas, I cherished the years that we had with our Dad. To this day, on certain anniversaries and certain dates I do things that remind me of him. I make a special meal that I know was one of his favorites—things like that. So, it has always been a turn *to* Jesus for me.

My parents introduced me to Jesus when I was little. I am a cradle [ELCA] Lutheran; I was baptized at the church my parents were married in and that my Mom grew up in. We were always at church; Sunday and Wednesday nights I was always there. I participated in the kid's choir and Confirmation. And I was a youth group leader in my teenage years—I was always at church. It was a good three mile ride and I rode my bike to church when my parents couldn't take me. I loved it, I was a church nerd.

My sexual orientation is its own journey. My decision to come out was a personal one. For a long time I was only out as lesbian, not as bisexual. When I first came out as bi I got some discrimination on both sides of the circle, both from the LGBT community and outside the community. So I took a step back and just said 'I'm part of the community' and everyone assumed that meant I was lesbian. I just went with it for a very long time because it was easier. I felt like I had to defend myself otherwise and I just wasn't ready to do that.

Church was a different story with a much better ending. I was at a Bible study the first time I came out. I was leading the Bible study at a local coffee shop and the discussion went to the topic of the LGBT community. Since I was not sure how they were going to handle it, I got up from the table and walked away. I went and hid in the bathroom, coming back to the table a few times to find the discussion still going, so I would go hide again. I figured it was my life we were talking about, even though they did not know at the time. Still, I was not ready to argue about it so I chose not to come out that night. To be fair, it was a mixed group of Lutherans and Baptists and that made it even more confusing for me. I was just not ready to deal with it.

The next weekend some friends and I went out to dinner before Bible study. They could tell I was a bit anxious so they trapped me in the corner booth at the restaurant and said, "What is going on?" I came out to them and thankfully they all acted like it was no big deal. So, it was no big deal. I was glad for that. Everyone assumed I was lesbian and even then I didn't correct it. Then I came out to my Mom on my 31st birthday and for her also, it was no big deal.

It wasn't until I started going to The Table that I came out as bisexual. The first time we sat down and had coffee together, you asked me what my sexual orientation was. I was so nervous about answering that question. Even knowing your story and knowing that you are bisexual, I still had a hard time saying that out loud to someone. Then a few weeks later another member said something about me being lesbian and there it was! I was quick to correct him saying, *"Wait a minute mister; not every woman in the LGBT community is lesbian."* He apologized and I followed up, "It's okay this time because you didn't know. But bi erasure[1] is real. It is painful and it is real. It is very real."

[If you knew Lexi, you would know that there was a gentle smile and a somewhat meek, comedic tone in her words, making this bold action quite sacred and beautiful.]

How would you describe your growth journey during your time with The Table?

The biggest thing for me is I did not have to "check who I

---

1. "Bisexual erasure," also termed "bisexual invisibility," is a pervasive problem. The existence and legitimacy of bisexuality is questioned or denied outright in many communities. The pain is very real. I may be too gracious in this area. I would like to think bi erasure is largely due to a lack of information, instead of the harmful act of denying someone's truth and delegitimizing their lived experience. The ignorance around bisexuality is similar to that of asexuality and intersex. Statistically however, there are more bi folks than any other on the *sexual orientation and gender identity* (SOGI) spectrum. Please do not tell a bisexual person to "pick a side." Instead, learn more information at https://biresource.org/

was" at the door. The church I grew up in was affirming. Most of the churches I went to as an adult were affirming. The church I left to come to The Table was affirming. But I still felt like either I was a Christian or I was a member of the LGBT community. There was not an overlap of those two things. I *checked* my "biness" at the door when I walked into church, and I checked my "church nerdiness" at the door when I went to an LGBT event. At The Table, I didn't have to do that. I could do things that were *churchy* and things that were *not churchy*. I could be in a space where I was totally and fully me. So, I was fully integrated. I got to be a whole person.

I was talking with the pastor here, where I live now. That was one observation he made when I talked about The Table. He said to me, "You got to be wholly you." And I agreed, "yes, I got to be wholly me"—with a W not with an H. I think I grew a lot in that because I just feel like you grow in general when you are allowed to be who you are. It opened doors for me to do all sorts of things and grow in ways outside of the church, even ways that have changed my life for the better. Learning that I don't have to give every last ounce of who I am—then run and find something to fill *my* cup. I can fill my cup *while* I am giving and there is a *balance* there.

I'm always going to be a caregiver. My profession now is caregiving. Learning how to live fully integrated with both parts of myself has taught me how to better care for myself too. For example, I have a 45 minute drive home where I decompress from one form of caregiving at work and get ready for the next form of caregiving at home.

I've been meeting with a health and wellness coach and have even changed the way I eat. I've lost 50 pounds in the last year. All of this stuff has been happening by taking care of me. At home we changed the way we cook. Each of them [mother and brother] cook one night a week now which even a year and a half ago wouldn't have happened. People who know me and know my relationship with my mom and my brother are just absolutely shocked that I have them cooking once a week and they're eating healthy with me.

I have been working with a new primary care physician since moving here and she has me doing all sorts of crazy things. She gave me referrals to new sorts of doctors to get my mental health meds under control and reduce a few to find a better balance. I have reconnected with friends I have known since I was five and have become more whole. So many things have changed in the last 9 months, it's crazy. This move came at the perfect time even though it was brought on by a whirlwind and toxic work environment.

I am taking all of the formal channels to do all the things that I need to help me live more healthy. A year ago I would have never done any of this, I just would have toughed it out and done what I needed to do to get through the day. So I think a lot of that kind of personal growth has come from my time at The Table and being able to grow into a person who knows their worth instead of their worth being based on everybody else's opinion or needs.

Describe the life cycle of the 3 R's in your faith journey.

Definitely the biggest for me is *reframing* myself. Being able to put myself into new situations when I would have run from them before. Being able to reclaim who I *am;* to be able to give back, whether it is back to my workplace or back to my family.

I did not come from a place where I felt like I needed the church to restore my faith or anything like that. I have had religious trauma but it was never a big enough thing for me, in the times that it happened, that I felt like I needed to *reform* to become part of the church in a different way. I think some of that is because I am bi and I pass for straight a lot of times and I can walk in and out of spaces without having to reveal who I truly am. People look at me and see a straight, white woman and that is not at all how I identify.

Being able to *reclaim* who I am through learning the 3 R's really has helped me change. And I feel like a lot of this change has happened since I've left The Table. The seeds were definitely planted while I was at The Table and while I was learning from you and from those around me.

[About this time, I had a eureka moment. During all of the interviews I have kept in search of the answer to 'why this person, Lord? What do they need to share to help themselves and others heal?' This right here was the answer. I thanked Lexi for sharing this detail and let her know she revealed something that had not come out in any of the other interviews. What I learned about Lexi is that the impact of the 3 R's was not so much on her faith life as it was on her personal life. Which is interesting when we overlay it on the lessons and stories in the Bible and the times that Jesus spent teaching life skills. I think sometimes we co-opt the lessons Jesus teaches about life skills as a replacement for what Jesus teaches about religion and faith.

Many Christians read scripture to learn about how to have faith. Lexi already had a solid faith and it is working quite well for her. What she needed to learn was how to take it from the pages of scripture and stand it up, so that it could have feet in her world; so that it could empower her, not so much in faith but in living.]

When I was church shopping around the area I am living in now, I went one Sunday to the Lutheran church five minutes from the house. The sermon had nothing to do with how to apply the scripture of the day to my life. It was all historical learning and I knew I did not need that. So I went to the next Lutheran Church in the area, ten minutes down the road. The pastor was preaching about how to apply what was in the Bible to your life today. That is the kind of church I belong in. I want to know *'how does this apply to my life? what do I need to do? how do I take this with me for the week?'* versus teaching me the historical context behind the biblical whatever. I am a church nerd, I have that part down already. I need to know *how* to take it with me down the road.

How did Pastor Dawn's leadership style differ from what you were used to or experienced with?

I think you are much more approachable than other pastors I have had. You are not sitting up in the ivory towers waiting to give your next sermon. You are on the ground running with us, working with us on whatever project it is. Your sermon style is very different from what I am used to. A lot of times I would go to church with my mom in the morning and then I would come to The Table at night. The sermons could not have been any more different. I often thought 'I got nothing out of the morning service where I got this, this and this out of tonight.' There were weeks where I felt like sermons were preached right *to* me and not always in a good way. There were weeks where I was really struggling with something and you hit a nerve; Then my whole therapy session would be just talking about what happened in church that week. It's why one of my favorite shirts says, "It's okay to have Jesus and a therapist too."

All in all, your sermon style is very different from others. But it had to be because you were talking to a very specific group of people, whereas most pastors are trying to cover all of their bases and make everybody happy.

[Surprisingly, Lexi struck a nerve in me when I heard this part of her story. I could have not spoken about it but that would be disrespectful to the project. Thoughts bubbled up that I have not verbalized out loud before, for lots of reasons. To that end, it is important that I embrace my vulnerability and verbalize them now: In the pulpit, there are preachers who phone it in; There are preachers who want to be liked, so they preach the easy, feel-good message. I would be a liar if I said I did not want to be liked also. But early on I realized the responsibility of being in the pulpit of an LGBTQ+ church.

In full transparency, the Church is the major cause of the breach for most LGBTQ+ folks. The Church (Institutional and local) has caused tremendous harm to the spiritual health and well being of many people in the queer community; It has done so much damage to our people group. This is why it is the Church's work to repair the breach and facilitate the healing.

I absorbed that responsibility then, and I absorb it today. What I tried to do was normalize us at The Table. I was very aware that we were a bunch of gay folks and that we have unique challenges; some of which are caused by the Church, some of which are caused by society due to homophobia, transphobia and over supply of societal -isms. Still, I always tried to normalize us as gay people; as average people who work for living, pay our taxes, raise our kids, go to school, go to the grocery store and mow the yard. We do the dishes, and do our laundry...these are normal, everyday things.

So, I tried to normalize us but not in a way that forgot that we have special challenges because of the Church. I always felt responsible to give us an extra dose of anchors to live our life by. Anchors that are rooted in our faith, our sacredness, our worth and value in God's eyes; Afterall, we are just normal people. We don't glow in the dark or levitate.

I do take my preaching responsibility very seriously. When I'm praying and studying, God is giving me stories. My responsibility is to deliver the stories. Some of the things I had to say in the pulpit, then and still today, are sometimes scary. There were plenty of times at The Table that I had to talk about the things that hurt us the most. Like sin.

Many in the gay community don't like the word "sin" because of the way the meaning of the word has been weaponized against their personhood rather than as a description of behaviors that separate humanity from God; A separation which everybody experiences. Sin is a universal thing. It is not a gay thing. It is an everybody thing. So I needed to remind us that we still need to continue to close the gap between us and God; And definitely NOT that it has anything to do with our sexuality or gender identity. Rather, we flubbed up in our *behavior and we treated someone differently than we knew we could. And to acknowledge we could have treated them better.*

Finally, I appreciate Lexi mentioning that sometimes her weekly therapy revolved around something that happened at church because I think it is a growth opportunity. Whatever "it" was that captured her attention, made her mad, hurt her feelings, made her doubt, stirred up something old or sparked up something new—Whatever "it" was, it stirred her up and kept her attention enough that she was able to take it to therapy.

Therapy is scalable. My therapist has an MDiv like I do. I am a huge proponent of mental health therapy.[2] It is a wonderful thing to be able to talk with a therapist and not have to check your faith at the door. And that is very unique in the queer community. It takes us having a solid faith if we have to go to therapy. If we have to check our faith at the door, we can choose to do that. At the same time, if we are standing on our own faith feet, we can take it anywhere.]

Is there something you learned or experienced during your time or your journey with The Table that helped your thinking and BE-ing?

I used to come early on Sunday nights. Most of the time it was just the two of us and we would sit and talk. Not necessarily pastoral care. We would talk about things that were going on at The Table, and what was going on at my work and home, and stuff like that. It was one of my favorite parts of my week—being in a space with you and having the ability to talk about whatever we needed to. There was no agenda to it, just two

---

2. It is advisable to seek a therapist with specific skills that most match your needs. Most therapists and mental health professionals are not theologically trained. If you suffer with religious trauma of any kind it is advisable to seek therapy from a spiritually educated and trained, mental health professional. Otherwise, a person runs the risk of further spiritual harm because the therapist will be advising based on their personal opinion and experience with religion.

people in the same room talking about whatever while we were doing whatever else needed to be done at that time.

[It's amazing what kind of healing and harmony can happen when you are folding bulletins; something that seems so basic and germane but wow, the healing that can come unexpectedly.]

When I came I was ___ and when I left I was ___.

When I came I was fried, for sure. I was trying really hard not to be, but I was not being fed in the space I was in and I needed something else. And when I left, I definitely felt loved.

When I said I was moving everyone said, "you can't leave us." It was funny because one person wanted to get up and give a speech about me leaving and I was not going to let that happen. It was funny, I could barely get out, "The whole world does not need to know." I very much wanted to take a quiet step out, and I was absolutely not going to be allowed to. They really wanted to acknowledge all of the things that I had done for The Table. It was nice that they wanted to celebrate me. So, when I came I was fried and when I left I was loved.

What is your greatest joy now?

One of my greatest joys now is being able to talk about The Table and tell people it existed. Chicago has a big Pride that is on par with Nashville Pride. Out here in the suburbs, everybody has their own little Pride that lasts for four hours on a Saturday or Sunday afternoon. So I have been to multiple Prides here. Being able to represent is fun. At one of the Prides I wore my WELCA[3] shirt, the ones we had made for our Chapter at The

---

3. WELCA stands for Women of the Evangelical Lutheran Church in America. More information is provided in Ginger's chapter.

Table.[4] Everyone was surprised and asked about a church showing up at Pride. I got to share and explain that this church was LGBT. Many people wanted to connect with us because they were so excited. I then had to tell them, "Unfortunately, it's not open anymore." So that was hard. Yeah, that was hard. And sad.

Even when I was talking to the pastor from my church now, one of his questions for me was, *where did you come from?* It felt empowering to talk about The Table and the 3 R's and how much I changed in my time there along with all of the positive changes I have been able to make since leaving there.

I think the other thing is the lifestyle changes I have been able to make in the last year including the weight I have lost. People who have not seen me in a long time are like, 'holy moly!' And now I can be supportive of others and encourage them: You can do it! You don't need to spend $8,000 [to get healthy]. I have literally been just walking and doing yoga online. Just being able to talk about those things is what brings me joy right now.

Is there any part of your story we did not talk about that you would like to share?

Earlier we talked that many people at The Table had a high degree of religious trauma. I made mention that I have not had a lot of church trauma in my life, this is true. But I *was* kicked out

---

4. One of the greatest achievements for me (Dawn) was being able to work with the ladies of the church as we formed the ELCA's first and only LGBTQ+ centered WELCA Chapter. WELCA is the Women of the Evangelical Church in America. Forming this uniquely crafted Chapter was quite an honor. We were able to share a lot of information in loving and caring ways throughout the country. You will read about Ginger later on, in Part III: *Ginger Widens WELCA*. This was a truly magnificent accomplishment for our church. Our women's group consisted of 4 transgender ladies, 2 bisexual ladies and 2 lesbian ladies.

of the church as a teenager. I was told that I did not belong, by an ELCA Lutheran pastor, in fact, who was an old fuddy-duddy curmudgeon. He said I was too forward thinking.

The church I grew up in had the same pastors from the time I was two years old until I was fourteen or so. After they left the Call Committee (a group tasked with interviewing potential pastoral candidates) was loaded with a bunch of little biddy women who wanted things to 'go back to the way they were;' Like in the 50's and 60's when 'the man was in charge.'

So they hired this ancient man, who probably was not as old as I felt he was when I was in high school, but he seemed ancient at the time. He shut down the youth group. He said we were not allowed to meet at the church any more because—of all things—he felt our youth group was "too exclusive," and [some] people didn't like us. On a weekly basis we had around 25 youth out of the 75 high schoolers who were registered as members or confirmed at the church. When we held a special event we would have 50 to 60 youth, so I never understood how the youth group was too "exclusive."

There were three of us in leadership at the time so we decided to talk with our parents. Since we could not meet at the church they allowed us to meet in our homes. Sadly, the curmudgeon found out and banned all three of us—banned us from the church. So, that is part of my story. I do know what it feels like to be hurt by the church. But it also taught me so many lessons about how to *be* the church without being *in* the church.

What would you like to leave as a public witness for others who may read this?

I think the biggest thing is just listen to where God's taking you. It may not look like what you expect. We have hardly talked about my leadership at The Table or anything else because of where the story went. And I think that says a lot about how the last year of my life has been.

I moved out of state before everything happened [the unexpected shutdown] because I was moving states away. But I still planned on becoming an online member. I was not going to leave The Table totally. I felt the loss just as much as the others because The Table had become my safe space. I want people to know, you never know what is going to make the change for you. Follow where God leads because you never know what is going to make the change.

HEATHER'S HEALING JOURNEY

"It wasn't until my baptism with the last gentle stroke of her hand, with that last sprinkle of water dripping down my face, that I would understand what she meant."

PASTOR'S PERSPECTIVE

On a rare occasion, God puts someone in your path who strikes you in profound ways. For me, there was not then and is not now, another person I have met who has had such complex religious trauma and an undying love for Jesus, simultaneously. That makes this particular chapter all the more tragic, frustrating, healing, and necessary.

One hundred percent of us, whether we are aware of it, or admit it, carry some religious trauma. Not everyone bothers to figure it out. Not everyone bothers to duke it out with God, with themselves, and with their pastor. For most folks with complex trauma, the journey to healing is long and winding. When added to this, the watercolor of religious dogma, hurt and harm, done in the name of God, quite often a person is left with a recipe for personal disaster. I learned that, in the South, there lives a colloquial phrase about kitchen spoons. It seems there is a relational difference between short and long handled spoons. Still, some recipes are hard to mix and they just need to be cared for with kindness.

I am so grateful Heather took a chance on herself and decided to write this entry. I know it has been a labor of love. I offered to her, as I offered to the others, the opportunity to interview and I would do the heavy lifting [because I knew just the telling of the story itself was a heavy ask] but to my surprise, she said she needed to write it for herself. 'It was a catharsis,' she told me. Like so many times before, I told her she knows herself best and I would respect her decision. Also, like much of our relationship, it was a back-and-forth, push-pull-sometimes-drag, yes-no-yes-maybe-no-yes vacillation. I finally said, this is it. You need to make a decision.

I'm so proud of her for not holding back. She was concerned that her chapter wasn't going to have a "happy ending." I quickly laid that manipulative thought to rest. I told her, "There is no happy or sad, or better or worse. It is your truth. Your truth is your truth." I encouraged her with every positive means of support I could genuinely provide, knowing that until I received the final chapter in writing, it may not see the light of day.

This is an important read, folks. I need you to understand, to the best of your ability, the depth of pain as well as muck and mire of emotional entanglement this lady willingly went through for you to see her gospel of Love and Grace, the pain of her crucifixion and the complete trust that she loves Jesus—despite what she has been told by friends, family, pastors, news, media, teachers and every other powermongering homophobic person you can substitute who claims that Jesus likely doesn't love her back. Religious trauma, like all trauma, is no respecter of persons. It is evil. And sometimes personified.

Over the years I spent countless hours in texts, emails, phone calls and visits with Heather, in my hopeful attempt that God would somehow speak through me to her hurting heart. It was months and years before I gained her trust; and even today, I'm not convinced she trusts me. She does believe that I have her best interests at heart, however. And that is enough for me. God will do the rest.

Heather, thank you for your participation. You are a powerful force of sticktoitness mixed with some vinegar and holy water. May the God of grace and mercy visit you daily.

(Note to readers: The interview questions are in a different order in Heather's chapter. I chose to let her story present as she wrote it. As is true to my chaplain nature, I worked arrangement around story, not story around arrangement. This technique is also a tool of trauma informed pastoral care (TiPC). There were a few questions I was unsure where to place, so I will let you discern that for yourself as you read.)

How did you find The Table and how did you find Pastor Dawn?

My journey began one night when I was working late doing some research on legislation in my state of Tennessee. As a social worker, I was searching for amendments to House Bill 1840 which reads, *"No counselor or therapist providing counseling services shall be required to counsel or serve a client as to goals, outcomes or behaviors that conflict with sincerely held religious beliefs of the counselor or therapist."* Tennessee was the first state to enact this law which represents discrimination against lesbian, gay, bisexual and transgender individuals. Tennessee has passed more anti-LGBTQ+ legislation than any other state since 2015[1]. Governor Bill Lee has been on the forefront of enacting legisla-

---

1. derived from *Movement Advancement Project*. https://www.lgbtmap.org/equality-maps/data_collection. doi 09252025

tion that restricts the rights and freedoms of the LGBTQ+ community.

During my research, I found an article about a pastor named, Dawn Bennett who was advocating against Governor Bill Lee for the LGBTQ+ community. I then began researching Reverend Dawn Bennett and reached out to her on Thanksgiving Day, 2021. I asked if she would meet with me so I could ask some questions. I didn't expect a response that day, or really, any response at all. Surprisingly, she responded to me that very day. She was in the airport and heading back to Nashville. She offered to schedule a day and time to meet with me. It was during my first meeting with Pastor Dawn, as I trembled with fear and uncertainty, that I learned about The Table. I was very forthcoming about my struggles and, along the way, would eventually share more of my life with her in confidence along the way. She understood me and was very relatable. I never felt judged by her. She understood my very deep abandonment issues and assured me she would remain available.

How did Pastor Dawn's leadership style differ from what you were used to or experienced with?

Pastor Dawn was unlike any pastor I had ever met. I was thankful that for our first meeting she did not wear her clergy collar[2]. We sat and talked for a while. I was certain that I was going to combust for even meeting with her, but she assured me that I was safe with her. Her leadership style was simple, "What do you need—we will build it, together." Over time and throughout deconstructing, my attitude became quite edgy, okay…I was an absolute brat. She had no issue with redirecting me when appropriate, but she did so in a way that I could never

---

2. for more description about trauma informed pastoral care revisit footnote on page 26.

stay mad. She knew I was deeply struggling internally without me ever saying it outloud. She would simply reach out a couple days later and check in, or I would quickly reach out and apologize. Over time, I would be apologizing quite frequently. Still, I always grew and always learned because she was patient.

What was the condition of your faith prior to joining The Table?

Prior to reaching out to Pastor Dawn and joining The Table, the condition of my faith was strong yet turbulent. From birth I was raised in a Charismatic Pentecostal church. I believed in and loved God with all my heart. I had a very strong religious foundation and faith. However, I only knew God as wrath and believed that I would be sent to hell because of my sexuality, which I really have no control over. My love for God has never been in question, though I never felt worthy; His love for me was always in question. I hated male pastors and churches altogether because I felt brow beaten every time I encountered one. I was questioning my religious upbringing, my personal beliefs, and my worth as a human. I was consumed with deep sadness, shame, and guilt over my sexuality. I had been contemplating ending my life. I struggled with that because I wanted to live. However, I wanted to live with peace in my soul, without mental confusion, and without religious bondage. Because of a very strict upbringing I didn't see a way that would be possible. I am a lesbian who desires to serve God, which isn't possible according to the church I was raised in. My soul felt restless. I prayed and cried out to God to help me. Then I found Pastor Dawn, my very first female pastor.

The Table itself was a unique church. It operated much like a community nonprofit with a spiritual twist, which piqued my interest, along with the slogan "all are welcome." Many churches claim that until you begin attending. The Table was where I found community and belonging; without going to a gay bar. There were other LGBTQIA folks who wanted to serve God. It encompassed folks like me – folks who were searching spiritually. The Table was where I would first be exposed to and immersed with the LGBTQIA community. It was a lot for me in the beginning. I struggled when I met the first transgender person I had ever encountered. I had a lot of questions, fears, and religious biases from my former denomination. It was then I learned something about myself. I learned that I love a person's soul and if I can do that, as a mere mortal human, surely, God does too. As I allowed myself to get to know everyone, I learned that we truly are all God's children. Each human truly is the face of God.

The Table always had something going on in the community and within itself. There were moments I was overwhelmed with all the things I was learning, and though my growth was quite painful, I grew. We were a family, and it was the first place where I was beginning to feel comfortable in my *own* skin. Still, due to my own religious trauma, I fought it every step of the way. Growth during my time at The Table was painful for me and I was a challenge for Pastor Dawn.

I was very suspicious, leery, and guarded. I was raised to be aware of "false prophets," so I did not trust her. I was raised to believe that I knew "the truth" and believing anything else would send me to hell. It would take me a long time before I could *really hear* Pastor Dawn's sermons. When I finally did hear them, it was very conflicting for me. The scriptures she preached were ironically the same, but her delivery, theology, knowledge and interpretation were very different. I questioned a lot because I came from a religious background where I was not allowed to question, at all. Pastor Dawn was patient and very gentle with me and my heart. She would constantly tell me that "I am worthy." She would tell me she admired me for never "throwing the baby out with the bath water" and instead, hanging on to God.

How would you describe your growth journey during your time with The Table?

In 2022, I found myself reluctantly agreeing to go to a Women of the ELCA Convention (WELCA), where Pastor Dawn attempted to stay close by me because she knew I would struggle. She'd softly whisper "lean in." It was during the first night of the convention where I would feel the Holy Spirit move throughout my soul, for the first time in a *gay-affirming* religious environment. I sat and wept. I didn't really know how to process my feelings. I was raised that the Holy Spirit could never dwell within a gay person because we are an abomination. I began weeping so loudly and uncontrollably that I left. I had to go outside to breathe. I was really confused about what I was feeling and what had just happened. The Pentecostals would say that I was *feeling convicted for being in sin.*

Pastor Dawn tried to journey with me during the convention, but I wouldn't allow her. Instead, I denied what I felt and numbed it out with a copious amount of Bacardi and Cherry Coke. I became very ashamed of that because I was at a church convention. To this day, I am not even sure if she knew or understood what had happened that first night. On the last day of the convention, Pastor Dawn walked down the aisle waving a rainbow banner while wearing her infamous rainbow converse sneakers – a pastor waving a rainbow banner under the instruction of the Holy Spirit upon her heart – I had never experienced anything like it. I was filled with a lot of emotions. As if I wasn't conflicted enough, it reminded me of a time when my mother waved the church flag in that same manner – for the church's beliefs and truth. But Pastor Dawn – she was waving that banner for us, God's children – the LGBTQIA+ community.

Although conflicting for me, after that I was beginning to see, feel, and understand God differently. I started to believe He was who He said He was and that is a God of love and grace, even for me. Perhaps, I was fearfully and wonderfully made, just as I am. Still, I could hear the Pentecostals' words echo throughout my mind from Proverbs 14:12-16, *"There is a way which seemeth right unto a man, but the end thereof are the ways of death."*

Describe the life cycle of the 3 R's in your faith journey.

Reframing, Reforming and Reclaiming (3 R's) would become a huge part of my journey going forward. I had a lot of scriptural hurt to undo, anger to unpack and a new faith foundation I needed to search for. I needed to reclaim my faith as a gay woman of God living in the Bible Belt. I couldn't do this alone, though I had attempted to convince myself I could, repeatedly. I finally admitted that I needed a pastor. It wouldn't be until 2023 that I was fully ready to embrace the 3 R's and begin very hard spiritual work. However, 2023 was also the year I became very sick and was hospitalized multiple times. Hospitalization would open many wounds of my religious struggles – "I am gay, I could die, I am very sick because I am being punished for being gay or taking communion or attending The Table, and I am so fearful of going to hell.' I was faced with the choice of a righteous Pentecostal male pastor who could get a prayer for healing through to God on my behalf, or I could take my chances with a bisexual female pastor who I was still leery of and not fully trusting.

I chose to take my chances and allowed Pastor Dawn to anoint me for healing, right there in my hospital bed. I allowed her to sit at my bedside and care for me. And when I was scared or crying, conflicted with fear over my soul, she was the pastor I reached out to. Each time. She always came to visit with me in the hospital regardless of what time it was. It was then that I *reframed* "pastor" and experienced something other than brimstone and fire. Fall of 2023, I began to trust her and allowed her to baptize me. She would always tell me, "I can teach anyone to float with just two fingers" and it wasn't until my baptism with the last gentle stroke of her hand, with that last sprinkle of water dripping down my face, that I would understand what she meant.

After that, I still had a long way to go. I was just beginning to learn to trust and hear her and learn God differently. I was just beginning to relax a little and trust myself in the decision I made in November, 2021. I had formed relationships with a church family – two of whom I had grown close to and who witnessed my baptism. I finally had community. I had no way of knowing that with that last gentle stroke of her hand down my face, that we would only be given one last year at The Table. I had no idea that my new church family would separate; That relationships would end for one reason or another and that there would be no time to resolve them. I had no way of knowing that the safe place I had found and the pastor I was learning to trust to journey with me would end abruptly in the most painful way possible.

The following year in 2024, I found myself becoming quite comfortable. I had never been to Nashville Pride because I feared Jesus would return and I'd be left behind. Still, I went. Even if it was only to help Pastor Dawn set up our tent for The Table. I was nervous and I recall snapping at a guy who was offering to help us with our set up. I didn't want to be seen because I was ashamed. I just wanted to put up that tent and leave. Quickly. Even so, I knew I was also brave because I was *at* Pride. I even wore my *'Bill Lee is a Drag'* t-shirt. Pastor Dawn was proud of my baby steps. She never pushed me or pressured me. Instead, she walked beside me along my journey. During a span when she was at the hospital completing a chaplain residency, I led many of our monthly Advisory Team Zoom calls and I enjoyed it. I was beginning to feel like I was part of something. I was growing comfortable in my own skin for the first time in my life. That is what was special about The Table, our gifts were always honored and elevated. We mattered.

In the Fall of 2024, Pastor Dawn went on a month-long sabbatical. During Sunday night worship services I found myself behind her pulpit, reading off-script, with a message of my own. In the palm of my hand I held the centering bell she would hold each week in the palm of hers. Sadly, she would never get the chance to teach me how to make it ring the way she was able to. It went flat with me. I was getting prepared to lead the Development Team and had some fresh ideas along with a new set of eyes to help The Table grow and expand. I was even ready to help carry The Table's banner in the 2025 Nashville Pride parade, a day I had worked so hard to be emotionally ready for, and a day that would never come.

In October 2024 The Table was closed abruptly and without warning. We all received a heart-wrenching resignation email from Pastor Dawn. None of us believed it. I don't even think she believed it. Something wasn't right. The sentence that stood out to me most, *"and now I must leave you."* I was flooded with many emotions that day, many I am still processing and working through to this day. The safe place I thought I had found, was gone.

The ELCA is no longer safe to me. I never saw The Table as a stand-alone entity. We were a Mission Development Church under the Evangelical Lutheran Church in America, in the Southeastern Synod. Yet, I saw us as a whole church family, as one. That is the way I was raised to see church. It is the way the Bible describes church, as one body, yet I felt very much abandoned and alone. I thought I had found safety and stability and a place that I could exist, just as I am.

I needed my journey at The Table and with Pastor Dawn to

be longer, because I have a long way to go. I have come so far and sacrificed everything, even my health. This is not a journey that I can do alone because deconstructing is extremely hard work and I require a pastor to journey alongside me. And not just any pastor, but the pastor that I was certain God and I chose, just for me. Over the next few months, I began to revert to the Pentecostal beliefs because I wasn't hearing Pastor Dawn's sermons anymore. The Table was closed. I had begun to see my former [Pentecostal] church family as protectors and was realizing that all this heartbreak is what they were trying to protect me from. I felt lied to and deceived. I felt like nothing more than an exploratory endeavor, an experiment for the ELCA. I no longer saw God's involvement in the decision I made in 2021, but deception by the enemy, which I fell for. I began to question my worth as a human.

I have started to be consumed with deep sadness, shame, and guilt over my sexuality, again. I hate male pastors and churches, again – all pastors really. I no longer know how to trust myself, trust a church, trust a pastor or how to prevent this journey from not being in vain. I don't know how to not be filled with regret. What I am certain of is that the Bible is a beautiful example of the way in which we should live and be toward one another. It is instruction on how to love and to be truthful, to forgive and be forgiven. However, it's also a book often used as a weapon to justify hate, and sexism, and to discriminate, to control, to judge, to condemn, and to separate us.

What is your greatest joy now?

I wish I could say that I have had some sort of epiphany and that all my hurt and trust issues over The Table's closure are behind me; that I am resolved and healed now. But I cannot say that yet. I hold on to faith that I will be able to, in time. I no longer have community, and I cannot write a happy ending about religion and my sexuality. Still, I did not leave empty; therefore, it was not in vain, though I must fight on the daily to keep it that way. I was left with seeds from my time at The Table. Seeds that I will hold tightly to, until I know what to do with them. I keep Dawn close by as my mentor and friend. She is the only pastor and anyone from the ELCA or The Table that I will allow near me. I no longer call her my pastor because she stayed with the ELCA, a denomination that I feel very much betrayed and deceived by. I'm learning to trust her again, slowly, cautiously, reluctantly and woundedly. But I am trying to take baby steps.

When I came I was _____ and when I left I was _____.

There are moments that I believe I am worthy. I still believe in God and have faith in Him. And I still have a strong religious foundation which is evolving into a spiritual one. I cannot be part of any organized religion at this time because I am afraid if I get too comfortable, the same thing that happened with The Table will happen again.

What would you like to leave as a public witness for others who may read this?

The biggest thing I have learned of late, is that we are all fallible humans, even bishops and pastors and church families. Even me. I often wonder if those who made the decision to close The Table have any regrets. Although, we may never receive full rectification for the hurt this has caused us or even the whole truth, we move forward knowing that what we found in that very special place once called "The Table" made an impact in each of us. We each grew and were changed for good, in one way or another. We will always be Pastor Dawn's imperfect little "ragtag band of misfits" that she loves, perfectly.

Pastor's Afternote:

Sometimes in writing, most especially when trying to present on behalf of another, I often am left with allowing structure, order and imagination to work its own magic. Because Heather needed to write her own chapter for catharsis and healing, I chose the placement of the interview questions. I did the best I could without changing her story, flow or truth. Speaking of which, truth be told, Heather's story is a fantastic representation of her faith: all over the map, many touch points, no end points, and a feverish tenacity to press onward toward growth and a deeper understanding of how God operates in her life.

May we all learn a thing or two...

CHARIS: TWO PK'S IN A POD

"I didn't seek God through you. I sought God myself. I don't rely upon you for my faith. My faith was my own before I got there."

PASTOR'S PERSPECTIVE

Charis' story is a bit different from the others. Her story really resonates more with my story. We share a lot of similar traits with some important differences. Growing up a PK (pastor's kid), if there is one thing that is weaved throughout your daily life, whether you like it or not, it is church. She and I have spent endless hours comparing stories of our PK childhoods.

Her Dad was a regional minister, so he covered a lot of churches with a lot of members, along with some added administrative responsibilities. Everyone knew him, therefore, everyone knew her. My Dad was a Deacon in the only Catholic Church on the four by six mile island I grew up on. Everyone knew him, therefore, everyone knew me.

I invited Charis to write with me because you need to know that stories exist for gay folks, that are not riddled with trauma and abuse *so deep that a person's life is shaken to its foundation. I asked her to write with me because stories like Charis's keep hope alive. If you ask her, I doubt she would consider herself a torchbearer. She's a pretty low-key kinda gal. Yet, I do suspect she would agree that her story is an important chapter in the larger story of 'God 'n the gays' (said tongue-in-cheek) because there are folks who are born into families where living somewhere on the SOGI scale[1] (sexual orientation and gender identity) is just another detail of their life, like any other detail. She is blessed in that way. Being gay, or in her case, lesbian, does not preclude her from the responsibility of being a kind, loving, helpful human though. Jesus was clear about that when He told us what was most important to him: To love your neighbor as you would love yourself.*

Because our stories are similar and details sometimes cross over, I chose to engage with her written chapter in real time. It makes more sense and I decided readers would benefit as well. I have learned a lot from Charis's silence. Most often she is a lady of few words, chosen wisely and spoken poignantly, when the time is right. Thank you Friend, I appreciate you more than I have words to adequately express.

How did you find The Table and how did you find Pastor Dawn?

I found you and The Table at the same time. Prior to the COVID-19 pandemic, I had been looking around and was aware of a few affirming churches. After visiting them, I found I wasn't really interested in what they had to offer. After COVID hit and the world shut down, we all had to stay home. When life began to

---

1. *SOGI Scale* is a later development in LGBTQ+ studies. SOGI stands for sexual orientation and gender identity. The SOGI Scale is similar in presentation to the Kinsey Scale. For more information visit https://www.apa.org/pubs/books/supplemental/Teaching-LGBTQ-Psychology/Activity2-1.pdf

open up again, I met up with one of our mutual friends [although we didn't know it at the time]; She wanted to go, and that night I went along with her.

What was the condition of your faith prior to joining The Table?

The title of the chapter kind of gives it away. My Dad is an ordained minister in the American Baptist Churches, USA (ABC). It's an interesting denomination in that most states have their own hierarchy which operates under the national denominational administration. I grew up in Michigan and Ohio where each state has its own executive branch that oversees all churches in their state. The polity, or church structure, begins with the Head who is the Executive Minister. Below that are Area Ministers, similar to a Bishop in the Lutheran tradition. They oversee the churches and are considered the 'pastor's pastor.' If a pastor has needs or personal issues they go to the Area Ministers for help. From there, each of the churches is, in a way, left to their own governance. They are autonomous congregations with some oversight from the Bishop (Area Minister). The makeup of congregational leadership in terms of racial, gender, and cultural diversity really depends on the church. There are some churches who will have a female pastor, others would not allow it. In terms of liberal or conservative, that really depends on how each church interprets the text.

Even though my Dad was a pastor, he was not my pastor growing up. He began his career as a pastor at a local church and before that he worked in youth ministry prior to becoming ordained. By the time I came along, we had moved to Michigan where he took a job as an Area Minister. He also oversaw the Camping Ministry in the state of Michigan. It was not camping like you would think of recreationally. Rather, it was church camp. We lived year round on site at one of the camps in Michigan.

Living in a camp setting provided a different way of life than most kids I knew. I think it was helpful for me to get to know myself, authentically. I liked different things than other girls around me, and I hated wearing dresses. I always knew I was *different* but I couldn't have told you why. At that time, there were other people in my life I knew who were also *different*. I just didn't have the language to tell you why.

Even though I knew I was different, it did not make my home life any different. At least not in a way that was troublesome. I was allowed to be me. It was the 80's and I was a tomboy through and through. I played sports and palled around with my older brother. We were often out in the yard playing ball or running around playing in the dirt. We lived out in the middle of nowhere, so life was a lot of being outside and playing.

I also love to take things apart. I wanted tools as a kid, no Barbies. I had a few Barbies, but it was more like Barbie and GI Joe. I played with both, usually together. Since it was just my brother and me, I usually got the toys I wanted. Not in a spoiled way but if I wanted a basketball, I got a basketball. If I wanted a doll, I got a doll. My toys were not regulated like, *you're a girl you're not getting that.* That was never a thing. In that sense, I never felt judged which is important. I think for a lot of our [LGBTQ] community that is a core struggle, particularly our trans* siblings who also knew that they were wired differently from a young age and didn't have language for it.

Earlier I said I had examples of things that were different. Being at the camp, I wasn't expected to be all frilly and girly. That wasn't the life we lived as a family. Not that I didn't have that example of my mother wearing dresses, I very much did. She was not a huge outdoors person but our life was in a Camp Ministry setting. I don't recall any of these specific details causing any issues. Yes, we had a very nice house on the camp property but we were always outside doing stuff. I was always walking around with my Dad or running around with the staff who were there. They were huge examples in my life.

Looking back now, knowing what I know, there were a few staff who were part of the LGBTQ community. Whether they were out at that time, or knew it themselves at the time, I do not know. But there was something that was *different* about them. No one really cared in the sense that you heard any kind of judgment. It could have been because they were not out. Again, it was the 80's, being out was not common for gay folks. Looking back, I can see how we were all *different*. To me, they were just the people I grew up with. That was us.

[Charis and I agreed that as PK's we look through a different lens. We agreed that we cannot compare ourselves, our upbringings, or our lived experiences with other LGBTQ+ Christian folks who didn't have a front row seat to church processes, religion, and family systems. As PK's we had a worldview that, whether or not we liked it, set us apart from most of our peers. Also, like Charis, I knew I was different but I did not spend all that much time trying to figure it out. I knew I liked boys and girls, equally. I was more apt to make sure someone was nice and kind than to concern myself with their gender. (I'm still that way to this day.)

I was not out when I was younger, even though I grew up in a Catholic Family filled with gay folks. I think, looking back, a lot of that reasoning is because I saw my brothers and my sister go through the coming out process and it did not go well. Also, I had no example of bisexuality represented around me, at least not that I knew of. Nobody in my family is Catholic any longer, except my devout Mother.

That is where my story and Charis's deviate. What we do hold in common is, as a Deacon, my Dad was always at the church. And I was always palling around with my Dad. I'd go to Knights of Columbus meetings with him. I often rode my bike over to the rectory to hang out with Fr. Pat and the priests. It was really common to have priests at our dinner table on the regular. Charis offered some of her own experiences too:]

I was around pastors a lot. On top of my Dad being a minister, my mother worked in the church office; the church we attended as a family. She started as the bookkeeper and then became the Administrative Assistant. I would go with her on sick days or when my Dad wasn't home. I would pack a sleeping bag and pillow. When we got there, she set me up in one of the classrooms and I would watch whatever *Greatest Adventure* cartoon or Christian movie they had around. I still remember those days with fondness.

Being at the church was never a punishment. We were there a lot, not just on Sundays. We went Wednesday nights for the kids programs and everything happening on the weekends beyond worship. I can still remember every hallway and every room...even the smell. It smelled like every other church you walk into. I don't even know what it is. They all have that same smell, it is like a combination of paper and old books and something else I cannot describe. Every church I've ever walked into has the same smell. And I've been to a lot of them.

My brother and I ran all around and we'd even go play in the nursery. It was just the two of us, running around in the dark. Even as young children we roamed all over by ourselves. The church was multiple levels so there were stairs to jump off and stairwells to hide in. We got to explore different places that most folks do not normally see a lot, like the baptistry and choir rooms. Church members usually only see those places once or maybe a few times. They were my playground. I have good memories about that time in my life.

With that firm foundation, it seems weird to say out loud but I have never really questioned my faith. It has always been a part of me. Growing up as a preacher's kid, in that space, being at church all the time, being around other pastors and always being surrounded by other people of faith, it was natural for me.

I gained very quick insight about what 'faith in action' looked like. What it looks like to be faithful to your core—to where you do not really question it, and it is just a part of who you are. So, even though I hadn't been attending church for some time before I went to The Table, my faith was very well intact and very much a part of who I was and how I lived.

I just always believed God was listening. I guess you could say I had certain expectations of God. Not that bad things wouldn't happen but that I was always going to be seen through it, and I was not alone. I have always had an expectation of God always being there. Even with my trials and hurts, I never saw myself as anything but coming out the other side. I take that back to always being surrounded by people who had an unwavering faith. Living like that unlocks so much in your life. I have always had good examples to pull from.

I know I walk in privilege. Part of what makes it a privilege is having that kind of faith from such a young age. I have had the understanding of a personal relationship with God and, maybe, in many ways it protected me from trauma that other people experienced at the hands of the Church. Several years ago I remember my Mom saying that she and my Dad set out to give my brother and me our own faith. They wanted to expose us to a wider world and let us experience faith, belief, and Christianity in a much broader spectrum than just one church and one pastor. I do not know how they accomplished it but that was their goal: for us to know who we were and what we believed, to our core. Speaking for myself, they managed to do that.

[Turning to me, Charis said] You and I have been around a lot of PK's over the years. And some of those stories are not good stories, I know. I think you and I are the lucky ones. Maybe not lucky but I do think we are the fortunate ones and I'm grateful for that. There are plenty of PK's who don't have a relationship with God anymore; who don't have a relationship with their

family anymore. That is something, unfortunately, that parallels a lot in the LGBTQ community.

When you get to focus on a personal relationship with God, not a relationship with the church, not a relationship with a particular pastor, but with God, you get to experience what peace looks like, what immense love feels like, what Light is out in the world, and you get to experience this *knowing* of God. It is almost indescribable. I can feel, inside, a presence. I can feel, inside, how to tell what is right or not. I can feel, inside, that what I am being told is what God is telling me.

I seek God myself. Even going to The Table, I didn't seek God through you. I sought God myself. I didn't rely upon you for my faith. My faith was my own before I got there. When you seek a personal relationship with God you open yourself up to actually hearing that 'still small voice.' I listen for however God is going to speak to me, whether it is the urge to do something or not do something. In my life, it is sometimes as simple as *how many times did I have to run back in the house to get something I forgot, and then maybe I am driving along and there is a huge accident* and I realize I am no longer mad about having to go back. It feels like maybe it was Divine protection. Yes, I was angry at that moment because maybe I had to go back in the house four times. Well, that was likely my ADHD, but still. For me, it can be as simple as that.

The first time I heard God speak directly to me was when I was really coming to terms with my sexuality. In that, He spoke to me and He told me I was okay; that I didn't need to worry about all the stuff I was worrying about. That I was okay as I was.

[I asked Charis if she felt comfortable sharing that part of her story, as vulnerable and delicate as it can be. She graciously agreed. Remember folks, this book is a love offering more than it is anything else. Every person who found Love and comfort and help at The Table are indeed blessed beyond measure. Charis has experienced something

that not many folks admit to. It is private. It was life-changing. It is also an important detail—she had already disciplined herself to have a prayer life, standing on her own two feet, not her dad's or her mom's or the staff counselors at Camp. She herself took on the responsibility to make sure she had a relationship with God. By her admission, she said it is all she knew, that she did not know 'any other way to be.' Yes, that is a blessing to her, laid foundationally by her parents. We are not all so fortunate. But Beloveds, by God's great grace, that building of a personal, private relationship with God, it is available to all of us. Full stop. No exceptions (no matter what ANYONE tells you).

I want to be sure to say thank you to Charis for this particular addition:]

I am not going to tell you the ABC churches are welcoming across the board. Many churches have left the ABC because they were not as welcoming as they could be. Again, when self-governance is on a local level they can do things like that.[2] But also, there are plenty LGBTQ folks who are part of ABC churches. I will say though, with the risk, a couple folks will stay quiet. I did not grow up hearing it was wrong or anything like that. Again though, self-protection by seeking God on my own and having my own faith, even if I had heard it, I probably would have dismissed it. Because I have listened for God from an early age.

As I shared earlier, I knew I was different. I didn't know why and it took me, honestly, till I was in college to really figure it out for myself. And even after that to really start to accept it. Then it came to a point where someone asked me about how my personal life was going. I said I hadn't found the right person; I didn't say man, I said the right *person*. I thought it was an

---

2. It is not only the ABC, USA Church. Most mainline Protestant denominations have had similar splits over issues concerning women's ordination, LGBTQ+ membership and ordination and the like. It would not be fair to isolate a denominational split to the ABC when most of us (churchs) have had similar fractures. The ELCA experienced theirs in 2009.

innocuous statement. But they picked up on it and basically told me I needed to 'stay away from that' and all the *stuff* that we [gay folks] have all heard on some level.

That's when it really came to me. I was looking, I was praying, I was going through my Bible, I was, for lack of a better phrase, trying to pray it away. I was trying to get all the answers to tell me this was wrong—that I was wrong. I remember sitting on my couch, Bible in my lap, praying and upset, and trying to figure it all out. Then, I heard God. Literally, all He had to say was, "You are okay," and that was the end of me fighting it.

It still took some time after that but that is when I stopped fighting. That is when I accepted that 'this is who I am.' I decided I needed to figure it out from there on because it doesn't matter what anybody else says, I know what God told me.

How would you describe your growth journey during your time with The Table?

I think my time at The Table allowed me time for curiosity and grace. Even before I came to The Table, I had been leaning into a concept of 'maybe it is not that simple.' And in it [the concept], it gives the benefit of the doubt, it gives grace. It allows room for curiosity. When you are looking at a situation, maybe you do not understand it, maybe you have a general reaction from the way you were raised, or that is not how you did it or how you grew up—just being able to take a look, a step back, and say 'maybe it is just not that simple.' Maybe it is not as simple as what I see it as.

That opened up a lot of things for me, in life and in general, but being at The Table allowed me to apply that [concept] in more of a faith setting. I didn't have all the same experiences other people had and I was faced with the reality that faith things could be different in terms of carrying religious trauma. I don't want to say I took it for granted but as we mentioned earlier, the privilege of having your own faith, of having a deeply personal relationship with God that is your own, and how that protects you from other things, at The Table I was faced with people that did not have that. That was a little bit of a culture shock for me. Not that I hadn't experienced other things like that before but to be in that Community with those people, it really gave me a chance to open up and find that grace. And also find that curiosity.

I think we all had that opportunity, the one that invited us into an exploration of grace and curiosity. I think when we go forth with that, we can leave judgment at the door. It is easier to stop thinking about how you are seeing it, what your initial gut reaction might be. You come up with understanding, or at least you are stepping towards understanding. So for me, I got to flex that a little bit more there [The Table]. My capacity for understanding really expanded. If my growth was in anything, it was in that, expanding my understanding.

Describe the lifecycle of the 3 R's in your faith journey.

For me, part of it is taking in that no one else's judgment is my responsibility. It doesn't matter what anybody else thinks, it's not my responsibility. The second thing is my faith is my own. It's between me and God. It is not up to, or dependent on, anybody else. The last is securely knowing I am who I am. I am blessed by God without apology, shame, or fear.

[Our discussion led to a follow up question. I asked her what she would say to someone who responded with some version of 'well that is all well and good for you, but you had parents who affirmed you. I had parents who didn't affirm me. So how can I feel secure? How can I believe that I'm blessed by God?' She responded:]

I think for most of us, on some level, even though I can say I was affirmed by my parents, when I eventually did come out, there was still a lot of fear. When it comes down to it, I am still a

Baptist Minister's child. That is not an easy thing to get past. Even though I was still pretty certain I was going to be okay, there was still some fear there. But my security is not them, it is God. So if you are looking for security, you go to God, not other people. It still may not be easy but that is where you start.

[Now, with my heart, I had to speak from a pastoral lens. I have had the privilege and responsibility to shepherd hundreds of people over the years. It is not a responsibility I take lightly, neither do I consider myself in any way a stand-in for God. I do however know I am educated, trained and skilled at communication, and have a theological understanding that has drawn me to a place of leadership. That said, I am a stepping stone. I will always redirect back to God. In addition to Charis's response, as a pastor I have learned some important truths.

The truth of the matter is, between all of us human people, not one of us really has it all figured out. Some of us like to think we have it figured out more than others. But at the end of the day, we do not. We are humans, we are not infallible. We are all taking our best shot at describing an indescribable God. We are trying to contain a God who absolutely refuses to be contained. So much so that God is going to pitch a hissy fit, in the form of Mother Nature, to prove the point that She will not be contained. Full stop.

I think this is where folks have become victims of other folk's theological worldviews. Instead of clinging on to the reality that there are just some things about God that are unexplainable. We've done our best to try to explain it, and in so doing, we have decided, we—we pastors, theologians, academics, parents to children, straight people to gay people, white people to people of color, Christian people to others— we've decided that we know best. That we have all the answers. And the truth of the matter is, we don't.

An important part of my ministry is to encourage and help facilitate a person's efforts to root themselves in God. It can be a hard thing for folks to trust when they have already been on the receiving end of hurt. I do my best to redirect them toward God, not me, not another person. 'God as they understand God.' Knowing that the longer we live, our understanding of God is going to change. But for whatever it is today, be rooted in that. Because that is enough for today. It is this rooting, this trust, the one Charis points to, that tethers us to our Creator. Charis continued:]

It seems like a really simple concept and it takes a lot of faith. It is hard to have faith in something (or someone) you have been told doesn't love you; that It is not all 'fire and brimstone.' It is hard to trust that *It* is something different than what other people say *It* is; and that is the hill to climb. But I do think so many people are willing, even though it is not easy. I do not think it is easy for any of us, I really don't. None of us is perfect. None of us have it figured out. It is not an easy task for me and I think it is not an easy task period.

And still, I have an expectation of God to show up. I have an expectation for God to be there. I think the hard part is when we expect It to look like this and It actually looks like that. Or, we expect It to look like this, and it doesn't but we do not know what It does look like because we have not had enough exposure. Again, this is where I consider it my responsibility to own my own faith.

One of the benefits of being a church camp kid is, I was introduced to God also as nature. Going back to my parents making sure I had more than one pastor and church experience, it was not 'four walls' for me. I was taught to seek God in everything. If that is [what most church camps would call] chapel in the pines or something like that; or when you're sitting outside, or around the campfire singing some worship songs or some silly songs, there is always the opportunity to seek God and to have that experience outside of the place you are "supposed" to have it [i.e. a four-wall church].

The 3 R's is an interesting philosophy. For me it is cyclical, it never stops. Something that might be *reframe* now can be *reform* or *reclaim* later. As I was sitting down to think about what it [the 3 R's] meant to me beyond The Table—what it looks like on a daily basis—I found that it really just depends on how you look at it and where you are in that moment. For me, I found a real beauty in the way that it evolves and moves.

How did Pastor Dawn's leadership style differ from what you were used to or experienced with?

I grew up in a church with a female associate pastor, so I had that example. But I am well aware that women pastors are not welcomed or accepted everywhere. I remember when we moved over to my grandmother's church, I was in Sunday School and a quiz went around asking if we thought women should be ordained ministers. Now, this is me, knowing that I had a female ordained minister previously, we are also talking in the '90s; every one in the room answered, "no." When it came to me I said, "I don't see why not." Of course, I already knew that was a thing, that it was normal, too, at least for me. I remember being a little shocked at the discussion because I knew their particular Area Minister was a woman and had been already serving for years. It was odd because the church denominationally said yes, but that local church said no. It made no sense because they actually already had a female in leadership. I do know, there is a persistent challenge to female pastoral authority. And, as expected, it is by [mostly] men.

I think for you [Pastor Dawn], in the experience I have had with pastors, at your core, you are a teacher. Not all pastors are teachers. You want people to understand. You want people to see for themselves. You want them to come and ask you the question, so that you can sit with them and go through it. You are very much a teacher, in how you preach and conduct yourself.

You are also very willing to lean in. It may be a vague statement but it is still very true for you. It doesn't really matter what the rest of the statement is, you lean in. You don't back off. You don't push things down and say, 'no we're not going to do this.' Instead, you go in for it. A lot of people get brushed off when they ask a question. You do not brush people off or brush them aside, not even in the uncomfortable or the hard. In all those things, you lean into it. You are with people as they go through those things.

The last thing I have to say, and I think this is where your biggest difference lies, is you do not see the things that divide. You see the common humanity in people. In many times where someone may be seen as "other" or "less than," I have never seen you do that to somebody.

Is there something you learned or experienced during your time or your journey with The Table that helped your thinking and BE-ing?

As simple as it sounds, it was the reminder of the importance of being part of the faith community. Even when one is already a part of other communities. The LGBTQ community is very much a community. And even when one is a part of that, there is still something very important about being a part of a faith community. Being a part of The Table helped remind me of that. It became a very intentional practice for me, just to allow myself to be part of that specific community again.

Faith communities are important. But somehow, in the queer community, we just don't think we belong there. I think a lot of it goes back to [the] trauma, bad experiences, etc. But there's really nothing else like it [faith community.] When I was thinking about the other communities I am part of, the hobbies that I love and the people I have met through them, it is wonderful and I would not trade it. But there is something different about the faith community. For me it is hard to explain. It almost goes back to that 'expectation of being there.' We are all coming together collectively as a congregation, as part of a faith community, waiting and expecting God to show up. But the irony is, God does not show up the same for any one of us. God shows up very differently for each person who is there waiting. There really is nothing else like it.

I can describe it like this: I play darts on Tuesday nights with a group of people. We all have the same experience. We are all there to see each other, have a little fun, reminisce, do whatever, but it is all relatively the same experience. That is not the story in the faith community. Every one of us can walk out of there with a completely different experience. Still beautiful. Still fun. Maybe challenging. Maybe even a little hurtful because you are reckoning with yourself. It is all the same place but a different experience for every one of us.

When I came I was _____ and when I left I was _____.

When I came I was healing. Life happens. I had things that I was healing from. When I came I was healing. When I left I was evolving. There was a lot of learning and a lot of growth and change in attitudes. Yes, I think evolving sums it up pretty well for me.

What is your greatest joy now?

My joy centers around growth. Growth in life. Growth in faith—in stepping into being the most "me" I've ever been. It is kind of like a kaleidoscope, always changing but still wondrous and beautiful.

Is there any part of your story we did not talk about that you would like to share?

I can say that Charis was more than gracious in this interview and there was no stone left unturned and no path she was not willing to travel with me. I think if you are curious about any other part of her story, you would do well to reach out to her for a chat.

What would you like to leave as a public witness for others who may read this?

The more I thought about it, the more I felt I needed to say what God has told me through the years; through my coming out, through all the different changes. And that is, God isn't telling you to change. They aren't telling you to struggle. And They are not telling you that you are sinning. God is telling you that you are loved. God is telling you that you are created in their image. And God is telling you that you are okay just as you are.

Pastor's Afternote:
Charis mentioned that her greatest joy centers around growth. She likened it to a kaleidoscope, always changing but still wondrous and beautiful. I love a good kaleidoscope. One of my greatest joys coming out of this chapter, Two PK's in a Pod, is that I did not anticipate the deep friendship that I would later cultivate with Charis. I did not realize, during our years together at The Table, what God was doing in aligning me, as the pastor, with somebody who is a member, but whose story is similar enough to mine that I had a safe harbor.

Pastoring The Table was overwhelming some days because of the degree of religious trauma that folks carry. Sometimes it was far and away so different from my personal story that I was left emotionally bleeding out because of my heartache for these folks—who I just love, Charis and me included. I always kept my professional boundaries of confidentiality intact and never did I take her friendship for granted at any step, but I also didn't have an expectation that a relationship would necessarily continue. And I have to tell you, my greatest joy is that I can look her in the face right now, with a big smile, and know that she is one of my best friends. I haven't had a lot of best friends in my life because my life is messy, I'm weirdly wired, I'm a gay pastor, I grew up Catholic, and my family, well—My story is just so funky that most people are like, 'Yeah, no lady, you are a little much.' I may be a little much, but I am also just me. My greatest joy is God's gift to me; that in God's generous love for me, I have developed a new best friend, and it is just so...[sighs], I cherish it.

PART II
LOOKING OUTWARD

Jessica's New Name
Christopher's Imagination
The Intern Now Reverend Wesley King
Lance's Search for Welcome

JESSICA'S NEW NAME

"I never wanted to be famous, I just wanted to be myself."

PASTOR'S PERSPECTIVE

[Content warning: This chapter mentions suicide.] I was so jazzed up for this interview. I feel like Jessica and I have been around the mountain together. We have been up, down, through, around, under and over. It has been a wild ride. We have sat together on opposite sides of the hospital bed and we have been interviewed and photographed together on the front page of the Washington Post. Now that is a story in itself.

Jess, I am so happy to know you. My heart breaks in two with every suicidal ideation or attempt. I'm so, so sorry you experience those traumatic interruptions to your beautiful life. I pray the Universal God finds a way to talk to both of us in a way that keeps us on this planet together. You have been a shining star in my ministry, and this world, and in this book. This effort would be so sadly different without you in it.

No matter what anyone says or does, Jessica, don't let 'em dim yer shine, illegitemi non carborundum, my dear, dear Friend.

How did you find The Table and how did you find Pastor Dawn?

Well, I don't remember exactly how I found you. At the time, I was in the Veterans Hospital in Murfreesboro because I attempted to commit suicide[1]. I had come out to my wife and daughter, and my family about being transgender. My daughter and my sister accepted me readily but my wife started preaching at me all the time and telling me I was going to hell if I didn't change my ways—if I didn't renounce being transgender. Pretty much every day I had to hear her little sermons about *going to hell* because of who I am. For me, divorce was not an option. So, the only thing I could think of to do was to kill myself and end it that way. That would have ended a lot of things for me, but…

Toward the end of my stay, the hospital asked if I had anywhere to go once they discharged me. I did not. If I went home, I would be walking right back into the exact same situation that caused me to be there the first time. Of course they agreed. I stayed in the hospital from March 4th to April 7th of 2020.

[This is the part of ministry that is often behind the scenes, between professionals who practice referrals. Jessica was led to me, and me to

---

1. The more trauma-informed phrase is *attempted suicide, attempted to take my life, attempted to die by suicide*. In honor of Jessica's willingness to be vulnerable and honest, I did not make any corrections. Not in the moment; not now. If you or someone you know struggles with suicidal ideaton or self harm, help is available. 988 is the Suicide Hotline. Don't believe the lie that your life has no value. You are loved. Your life is sacred.

her, through the Chaplain at the Veteran's Hospital who knew of my ministry and advocacy work with LGBTQ+ people. The Chaplain emailed me to inquire about a referral. That is how Jessica and I met. I was not able to visit her in person because of the pandemic health restrictions, however we did talk on the phone. I did not offer this up during our interview because those details are part of my story, not hers.]

After I was discharged, I recall looking for your sermons online so I could listen. When we were allowed to meet in person I decided to come over on a Sunday night.

I introduced myself the first time I was there and you were so accepting. I remember thinking *this is a person I would want to be friends with*. That is what I can remember. Most of what I remember from back then is taking half a bottle of ibuprofen and having my stomach pumped at one hospital and then being transferred to Ward A, the psych unit, at the VA Hospital.

This question led us off down a path I chose to include for advocacy purposes:

Dawn: *We have come a long way and I am very, very thankful that whatever amount of Divine Providence was in play, that we are here to talk together more than 5 years later. The Table started in January 2020. I was online preaching from my living room because of the pandemic; we were still trying to figure things out - there were no people, there was no church, there was nothing.*

Jessica: I am so glad we found each other though. There are not many people, much less friends, that I can say, "I love you" to, but you are just such an amazing blessing to me and I love you very much.

Dawn: *I love you too. It is a real blessing to have people like you in my life. It helps keep me grounded and hopeful. Part of what I do not talk a* *lot about in my story is that I have a transgender son in his 30's. He has dealt with suicidal ideation; he has dealt with depression; we have had those hard conversations. He is ten years into his transition now. To my knowledge, he has never attempted to take his life. Being in relationship with you and other older trans*[2] folks at The Table helped me develop a sense of hope for my son. You are old enough to be his parent, so it gives me hope that there can be a vibrant future for him. It is like what we tell a lot of the younger kids, 'we need to keep you alive long enough for you to experience it.' You have been helpful as a source of hope running in the background of my personal life, as the parent of a trans man.*

Jessica: I always wondered what it was like for you to be the parent of a transgender person because I know what it is like to be transgender, what it is like to grow up that way. I knew it when I was 9 years old. I didn't know the word *transgender*, or anything like it, until I was in my fifties. Still, I knew what I was. So to be the parent of someone who has probably known for most of their life as well, I have wondered about that.

Dawn: If you ask my son he will say he has known all of his life, yes. He and I did an interview a while back and I asked him when he knew he was trans. He said 'as soon as I learned what the word meant, it was like a puzzle piece fell into its place in my mind.' He said it answered so many of his questions.

Jessica: At times, I wish things could have been different, like maybe I could have been born thirty years later. But at the same time, going through what I went through growing up, that is

---

2. Trans* = there is "no one right way" or "only one" way to "be trans." Transgender is an identity that is as diverse a spectrum as many other identities. The most honorable way to engage a transgender person is to ask them how they identify, ask them what pronouns they use. If all else fails you, call them by name.

what made me the person I am today. Like your son, until I found the word *transgender* and learned what it meant, I didn't have the language for it either.

What was the condition of your faith prior to joining The Table?

When I found The Table, I was in a really bad place spiritually because I had been in the church since I was born. I grew up first in the International Fundamentalist Baptist (IFB) church. After we moved to Tennessee in 1968, we started going to a Southern Baptist church. From that point on, all I ever heard about was *what a bad person I was because I liked boys*. I grew up calling myself *gay*. I never heard the word *homosexual* until I was about thirteen or fourteen. I had no idea what that was. I didn't know what *gay* was. I just knew that I liked being with boys.

My parents took me to a child psychologist in Knoxville, Tennessee in 1974. Instead of meeting in an office, the psychiatrist asked me to go on a walk. The very first question he asked me was, *do you like having sex with boys*? I immediately decided, *'I don't know this person. I never met you until 5 minutes ago. I am sure as hell not going to tell you what I am thinking about sex. I do not even tell my parents that.'* I do remember asking him what a homosexual was because *he* had used the term. He told me it was someone of a gender who liked having sex and was attracted to people of the same gender. I then asked him, what would you call someone who likes persons of the opposite gender and he said that is a *heterosexual*. I said, "Well, that is what I am." As I said, ever since I was 9 years old, I considered myself a girl. I know what *parts* I had, but also in my mind, I was a girl. After I told him that, he said we were not getting anywhere and the talk ended. We went back in and he had a conference with my parents. They never brought me back there.

That being said, I was Southern Baptist until I went into the

Air Force. When I got to basic training, chaplains from different denominations came to talk to us. The Mormon church chaplain said their services were three hours every Sunday, from one to four o'clock. He asked how many of us were Mormon, I raised by hand. Mainly because everybody else was coming back from chapel about the time I was leaving, so that meant I did not have to do any barracks details.

After I got out [of basic training] I made it to Minot, North Dakota. A friend who went to the local Assemblies of God church invited me to go with him. I had just gotten off duty and was covered in grease. He said he would wait on me. From there on, I attended the Assemblies of God church, even after I was discharged and returned to Knoxville, TN. I stayed in the Assemblies of God until I was about fifty. I had gotten married in 1992 and both my wife and I attended the Assemblies of God. Her uncle was an Assembly of God pastor, so she was very heavily indoctrinated into it.

If I thought I heard a lot about being gay in in the Southern Baptist Church, it was nothing compared to Assemblies of God. I even took some courses in order to become a licensed minister. The teaching was just too intense and negative about sexuality and it burned me out. So we started going to a Word of Faith Church here in Nashville. It seemed like every time I changed denominations it just got worse.

By the time I found The Table, I had been kicked out of a Reformed Baptist Church because after I came out to my wife and family, I went to the pastor. He said I could continue attending as long as I did not tell anybody about my gender identity and that if I continued to attend I could only wear men's clothes. He also forbade me from talking about my life with anyone else and I was not to bring it up to him, either. If somebody were to ask, I was to deny everything. I said, "And if I refuse to do all that?" He said, "Then you are not welcome here." So I was between churches for two or three months.

When I found you at The Table, it was the first time I ever heard anybody tell me that God loved me just the way I was. That He made me this way. And They [God] were not in the least bit upset with me for just being myself. That made a huge difference. Still, when I finally found The Table, I was an atheist and very angry at God.

I remember talking to you about it in your office and I said that sometimes I just want to yell at God and tell Him to fuck right the hell off. But I can't do that because I'm afraid of hell. And I'll go to hell if I offend God. And you told me that you cuss at Him all the time. That He's a big God and He can take it. *(Dawn: Yes, I did say that.)*

That was the very first time anybody ever told me that. To this day, I don't know if I still would think of myself as Atheist but I definitely don't think of myself as Christian. I'm somewhere on the Agnostic scale.

[I say this as a denominational pastor, I think agnosticism is probably as close to an Orthodox spirituality as we can get. We have not labeled God anything; we have not tried to box God in or paint God a certain color. We have not put a certain set of words in God's mouth. God is just God, the Sovereign. God is not happy, or sad, or mad, or straight, or gay, or shorter, or taller, bald or curly haired. God just is. God is balance, Universal Balance. Balance is germane, it does not lean in any one direction except in an attempt to level itself. And I think for many agnostic people, just acknowledging that there is something bigger than them in the world, that is enough. That is enough. Just knowing that I am not alone, that I was brought into this world with purpose, that is enough. Jessica continued:]

In the last five years I have been learning that God is not interested which hole you fuck in. He does not sit there watching you masturbate. As for my purpose, I have learned that one of the best things about being agnostic is deciding for myself what my purpose is. It never felt right when pastors would say *God has a purpose for your life!* I think God does not want shit to do with my life. He created me and gave me a brain to think with and to reason with. I get to choose my own purpose and that purpose can change from time to time. I do recall somebody saying that there are theists and there are atheists. Between the two, there are Gnostic theists and agnostic theists; Gnostic atheists and agnostic atheists.

So I have been trying to figure out exactly where I fit in there. Am I an agnostic-atheist or am I an agnostic-theist? Sometimes I do feel like there has got to be something or someone bigger than me because I have tried to off myself too damn many times and it has not worked yet. I am still trying to figure out where I fit spiritually. It might be another five years before I figure it out. I may never figure it out.

How would you describe your growth journey during your time with The Table?

Being at The Table really helped me to grow as a person and to accept that maybe I was wrong. I was a gnostic atheist when I met you [Pastor Dawn]. I just knew there was no God. For me, there could not be. Now, I have grown to the point that I know I fit somewhere along the agnostic spectrum. Five years ago that just was not the case. I tell people that it is really kind of bizarre that I am agnostic and that one of my favorite people is a pastor in a Lutheran Church. It is crazy for sure.

One of the things that helps me is the fact that you do not judge anybody, you just accept everyone as they are. For fifty-eight years of my life, I never had that. All I ever had was people who wanted to change me. And if I refused to change, then condemn me. When I finally met someone who was nothing like that, it turns out that she just happened to be a pastor, and bisexual herself.

I feel like I am morphing into something, I just do not know what that something is. I have been in therapy since last August trying to figure that and many other things out. It is a slow, steady journey. One of my favorite songs is one that Miley Cyrus came out with years ago called *The Climb*. Basically, the song says it does not matter where you have been, what you have been in the past; it does not matter what you are now, it does not matter where you think you are going because life is all about the climb. *(Dawn: I resonate with that very much, too.)*

Describe the lifecycle of the 3 R's in your faith journey.

Let me take the first one, *reframe*. Until I found The Table, I had never thought of myself as really being loved by anyone, much less God. All I ever heard was *you are a lowdown, no good, dirty, rotten sinner; and unless you do this [repent] you are going to hell. Or, if you do [that] you are going to hell.* That is all I ever heard. When you came along and put it in my head that God loved me exactly the way I was, I had never really thought of that. In fact, even during the time I was going to The Table, it took me a long time to claim that. Because once you have been brutalized by the "Christian" Church, for decades and decades on end, it takes a while to get it out of your head because you are still thinking the other way. I finally did come to a place where I can say, if there is a God, then that God loves me just exactly the way I am. For me, that was *reframing* and *reclaiming*.

It is good that *reform* is in the middle, between *reframe* and *reclaim* because that is the transitional word between the two. First, you have to learn how to think of yourself in that way [as you are, different and holy, sacred and created with purpose, in the gender identity and/or sexual orientation you know innately to be true for yourself] and then you have got to learn how to think of yourself as whatever it is you are. In my case, it is a transgender lesbian. For the longest time, I could not even begin to imagine God not being upset by that. I thought the whole LGBTQ community was on its way to hell. At least that is what I heard and learned from every pastor I ever had, until you.

I really think that *reforming* is the transition word here. It is the one that gets you from *reframing* the way you think to *reclaiming* who you truly are. That is the ladder that gets you up.

How did Pastor Dawn's leadership style differ from what you were used to or experienced with?

For one thing, in the last forty years or so, every pastor I ever came in contact with is all about the Benjamins. They are always preaching *'pay your tithe and your tithe is not your offering, so you need to pay both.'* Then there are churches like the Mormon Church with over $140 billion in the bank who preach that if you do not pay your tithe you are not going to go to Celestial Glory, which is heaven for Mormons. And the reason you are not going to Celestial Glory is because to do that, you have to go to the Temple. In order to get a Temple recommend[3], you have to pay your tithes. And—No, God does not want you drinking coffee or hot tea. And no sexual sins. If you are a teenager and you masturbate or you are having sex with someone, you have to tell your Bishop because you have got to repent of that. Until you do, you cannot get a Temple recommend. And of course, without that Temple recommend, you are not going to Celestial Glory. It just seems to me that in addition to telling people how to live, they also want to tell you how to give your money.

Then there are all those sermons about sin that I have heard my whole life. *'Everyone is a sinner, there are none righteous, no, not*

---

3. A temple recommend is a certificate for members of The Church of Jesus Christ of Latter-day Saints (LDS Church) that authorizes them to enter a sacred temple. To obtain one, a member must be interviewed by their pastoral leadership who assess their spiritual worthiness and commitment to the Church's commandments and definition of faithful living. More information can be found at https://www.churchofjesuschrist.org.

one. Everyone is a sinner, you were born that way.' Even though the Bible says that children are not supposed to be held responsible for the sins of the fathers. But God is God and God can do whatever the bloody hell He wants to, so he is going to hold it against you because Adam and Eve apparently sinned. So He [God] is going to make sure everybody else is a sinner too.

I never heard you preach a sermon about money. I never once heard you preach a sermon about sin. What I did hear you preaching about was the one thing I almost never heard in any of the churches I ever attended up to that point, and that was about love and forgiveness. That to me, is completely different from how I grew up.

[I could not let this moment pass without addressing it theologically. Truth be told, I did preach about sin and money and a host of other topics that have been crammed down the throats of unsuspecting, beautifully devout believers. Jessica, in her grace, gave me the space to share about my philosophy of sin:

There were many times I preached about sin, but I didn't use that word. At The Table I used to preach about the "gap" between our hearts and God's. (Jessica: Yes, I seem to recall that.) And how our daily aim is to close the gap, so that we can be one with God. All the time, every day. It was not a magic trick or hard puzzle. You do not have to close your eyes and go over here and do this [particular thing]...that God is just with you. Period. It does not matter if you are in bed with your partner. Or if you are in the shower. Or if you are at the stove cooking dinner, or whatever. God is with you. And that also, we are aware that we are not our best self 100% of the time; that there are opportunities to close the gap, so that we can have our heart be one with God's. That is how I would have talked about sin. It is still how I talk about sin.

My understanding of sin is an acronym, Separated In Nature (SIN). In my understanding, that is what we are—we are separated from God when we are "sinning." We are separated in our nature-sense from God because we are [insert "crime" here]. We are judg-

mental and all of those things that are not fruits of the Spirit[4]. *We have an opportunity to look at our behavior and make some corrections, yet we don't take it. But I do not agree we have to be bludgeoned to death for it. That is pointless and fruitless. There is no apology in that. It is not about shaming and guilting people into behaving. It is about conscientious objection, and having a moral compass that helps us be our best and do what Jesus said, which is treat people the way we want to be treated ourselves. It is a pretty simple philosophy.*

As pastor of The Table, what I always tried to do was meet people where they are, not bring them where I needed them to be, or wanted them to be, or hoped for them to be. No. It is not my life, it is their life. It is my role to meet folks where they are. Then, I am going to ask you what you need and how I can help you. It does not do either of us any good for me to give you what I think you need. What if I am wrong? My role is to ask you what it is that you need and go from there. That is what made sense to me. It is what still makes sense to me. And thank you, Jessica for giving me the space to explain myself.]

Is there something you learned or experienced during your time or your journey with The Table that helped your thinking and BE-ing?

One of the things that helped me the most was the transgender support groups. Being able to talk with other people, to hear their perspective and what they went through to get to where they were at that point. They helped me a lot, to understand that I was not alone. Even though there were many differences between us, we also had many things that we shared. I was really sad when we had to discontinue that group.

[*Because I know her journey, I asked Jess if there was anything else after the support group? I made mention of the photographs on her*

---

4. The *Fruits of the Spirit* are love, joy, peace, patience, kindness, goodness, faithfulness, gentleness, and self-control. Galatians 5: 22-23.

fridge and that some of them are pretty telling, like the one of she and I, where one could not manufacture the laughter we share." Jessica continued:]

It is one of my favorite pictures. That is the one that says to me, *this is how far I have come.* There was a point, when I first started at The Table, I did not like much back then. Being at The Table and being able to *come* as myself, and *be* myself, and not have to worry about anybody, what anyone else thinks, or is going to think...It was all about being myself and that allowed me to open up.

Even now, I do not go around telling everybody I meet that I am trans or lesbian. But if somebody walks up to me and asks me if I am trans I do not lie to them. Now, one of these days, I might do that and a person is going to have a gun in their back pocket and they might want to use it on me. But I am still not going to back off. I do not care what laws they pass or what executive orders get issued. I spent fifty-eight years of my life being in the closet and I will be damned if I am going back in now. *(Dawn: Amen to that.)*

When I came I was _____ and when I left I was _____.

When I came to The Table I was all bottled up. I had made up my mind that I was going to be myself by then but becoming that, that was the hard part. Being open with people about who I am is hard. That is why I immediately said yes when you invited me to do this project with you. I don't know, there may be somebody else who needs to know that there is hope and that you do not have to stay the way you are.

You can be yourself. It is not easy. Sometimes it is really difficult but the most rewarding thing you can do for yourself is just to let yourself be who you are. And if you need time to grow into that, fine. I have been growing into it for the past five and a half years. Probably in five and a half more years down the road,

I am still going to be growing. So, when I came to The Table, I was all bottled up and when I left, I was more of myself than I had ever been in my life.

What is your greatest joy now?

I always tell people that I like wearing makeup because it makes me feel pretty and that makes me feel good about myself. I enjoy that. What brings me the most joy is being around people, whether they call themselves Christian, or atheist, or a *none*. Whatever they choose to call themselves, just being around other people who share commonalities with me. I very much enjoy being *out* to the world, so hopefully somebody will come to me and say *'how did you do this? because I'm scared to death.'* I try not to tell them, *'well, I have been out for five and a half years and I am still scared to death.'* That is why I have pepper spray on my lanyard.

[That is just being a smart single woman in the world. Let's face it, it is hard to go out and about as a single woman. I also want to be transparent and honest and say that trans women are always in danger; trans people are always in danger. I think trans women more so than trans men because they are usually larger in frame. Trans women are often quite tall also, making it more challenging to blend in a crowd.]

That is why I have pepper spray. I have two; one is in the basket on my walker and the other one I keep hanging around my neck. I make sure that I have quick access to it because if I feel threatened, somebody is going home with pepper spray in their eyes.

Is there any part of your story we did not talk about that you would like to share?

My name change experience. I was so blessed to have you

with me that day. I was doubly blessed to have the magistrate I did (the Honorable Anne Martin). I was really nervous about going into the court for that. For the simple reason that whenever you fill out the application for your new name, they ask you why you want to change it. I told them, I have never felt like my given birth name. I have never felt like it fits me, and I am transgender. Her Honor asked me how I came up with my name. I told her the story: My first name came from the first woman I ever saw naked in a Playboy magazine . She was 5'8". I do not remember her breast size, I just knew that they were beautiful and that is what I had been praying for my whole life. My other names came from a high school flame I had a crush on, and then of course my last name is after one of my favorite country singers. She has one of the most inspiring life stories I have ever heard. She is proof that one does not have to come from music royalty to become music royalty.

I decided there is no reason why, if she could grow up in a literal shack in the hills of Kentucky and become one of the best known country singers and writers of all time, why could I not do it, too. I never wanted to be famous, I just wanted to be myself.

What would you like to leave as a public witness for others who may read this?

First, do not be afraid to be yourself. Whether you believe in a God or not, there are people who love you for who you are. And the people who do not, who want to change you, they are not worth wasting your time on. So, be yourself. Allow yourself to be who you truly are.

And the second thing is, you are loved. If you believe in God, believe that God loves you just exactly the way They made you. I know that for a big part of my life, I think even the last twenty years of my marriage, I wanted to be loved for who I truly was;

and because I was not, I was so busy trying to be who everyone else expected me to be. I became miserable. It was not until I allowed myself to walk in my truth that I was actually able to accept love from my friends and relatives who did love me. I do not know if I will fully ever believe in God again or not, but whether I do or not, there is somebody who loves me. And somebody loves you. Concentrate all your efforts on those people.

Pastor's Afternote:

There is something to be said for sitting in the presence of wisdom. I have had a lifelong pattern of surrounding myself with folks who are older than me. Perhaps because I am on the tail end of the six-kid birth order. In my life patterns I have sought out older, and in my opinion, more mature, people because to me it is a way to work history, wisdom and advice into my current lived experience.

It took me until Jessica's last sentence to inch a tiny bit closer to my own truth. I am an ordained Lutheran pastor. I am a pan-bisexual person of female cisgender experience. I am the daughter of a devout Catholic mother, whom I trust loves me, but also with whom I have struggled to have a close, intimate relationship most of my life. I know beyond the shadow of any doubt that my mom loves me. One of my siblings puts it best: Mom loves all of her kids; she just doesn't like some of us (reference to the gay ones, of which I am one.)

I may not have "wasted" much of my time trying to seek my mother's love or acceptance, that is true. I have, however, felt the disconnect for all of my life. I could say it is because she favors the boys (not untrue), I could say it is because I left the Catholic Church (not untrue), I could say it is because we have lived miles apart for all of my adult life (not untrue), and I could say it is because I have never once heard her utter the word bisexual (sadly and painfully, not untrue).

Not one time. Whether in general or in reference to me. The pain of that reality is...real.

Thank you Jessica, for sharing your story and for helping me resituate myself in my own world as a person with children and grandchildren who love me (and tell me and show me) and friends who love me (and tell me and show me). I have siblings who love me (and tell me and show me) and I have a congregation who loves me (and tells me and shows me). I do believe, with my whole heart, my mom loves me and that she does the best she can to tell me and show me. I also believe I will never hear her audibly acknowledge my full experience. One thing is for certain, I do believe that God, my Creator, did a fantastic job with my personal recipe and made me in a way that is like no other. And for that I am grateful and blessed.

CHRISTOPHER'S IMAGINATION

"I have so many layered memories of my time at The Table — some joyful, some uncomfortable, all of them transformative."

PASTOR'S PERSPECTIVE

Chris Flor is magnificent. It was the first word to come to my mind the day we met. It is a word that continues to come to my mind when I think of his artistry. He is one of the most creative and dedicated thinkers I have come by in recent years. I know he handled me with kid gloves, as my tech skills are more than lacking. I doubt that he would be willing to admit that in writing; It's okay, I did it for you! Were it not for him, streaming worship services at The Table [I am positive] would not have grown to the extent they did. Christopher, I will forever be grateful.

Chris and I love the same kind of music, we went to the symphony and secretly ate ice cream and cookies together. He taught me the importance of laughter. He also showed me what it means to be dedicated. Chris works in the school system. He advocates for students with all types of challenges: learning, behavior, home life, etc. He's a smooth operator and I have [from a distance] prayed for this aspect of his presence in the world, most especially for LGBTQ+ students and students of color, who are always over policed and underserved. But not on Chris's watch. The schools are blessed to have you, Friend. Keep on keeping on.

I remember when he first began posting on socials for the ministry. One time in particular I will dub "pulsating Jesus." Full confession: I do not have an eye for art or for creating graphics. I am a wordsmith. Christopher on the other hand—well, check out Queer Critical Faithful on Insta and you'll see! One night I asked him to make some graphics to go along with what I was preaching on. I set him loose and said (which I was all too famous for saying), "just use your imagination."

Okay, picture it: slightly psychedelic in nature, lots of vibrant colors, some neon, Jesus' face and a cross all expanding and shrinking from small to large and back to small.—I didn't catch myself in time and I [think] I said, "Chris, this is worship, not Vegas." From that time on he blessed The Table with his vivid imagination. Somehow in his savvy he took sermon snippets and created pentimento[1] artwork. Speaking of which, when we closed he blessed me with his first original composite of Blessed Mother Mary. It brought me to happy tears.

Chris was another person who chose to write his chapter for catharsis. I have to admit, I was brought to a different kind of tears, in a grateful, humble and lovely way. Thank you, Christopher, for your continued friendship and collaboration. May the God of Infinite Creativity be upon you and QCF as the Spirit would have it to be.

---

1. "*Pentimento*" is a process of canvas painting made popular in the Renaissance. In painting, a pentimento is the presence of earlier images, scenes, or forms that have been changed and painted over. For our purposes, Christopher seemed to almost magically weave scripture words and images together in a way that only he could. For more of Christopher's work check him out on socials at https://www.instagram.com/queer.critical.faithful/

How did you find The Table and how did you find Pastor Dawn?

I still vividly remember the first few times I heard about Pastor Dawn and The Table. One of the earliest moments was when Vanderbilt Divinity School published an article celebrating the ordination of the ELCA's first queer pastor in Nashville, TN. My friend Kim, who had attended Divinity School with Pastor Dawn, mentioned her name to me then. A few months earlier I had just started attending another ELCA Lutheran church downtown. In those early weeks, I was cautiously trying to discern how truly inclusive the community was. The downtown church's website offered encouraging signals but mostly used coded language—not bad, but not fully affirming either. One particular week the pastor spoke about attending the ordination of a local queer pastor colleague. He mentioned that the Sisters of Perpetual Indulgence[2] were there and emphasized his commitment to making the downtown church more inclusive. That sermon was a turning point for me. It helped me trust that I was in a place where I could belong and get more involved.

Soon after, the pandemic hit and everything changed. During that time, I developed a strong relationship with the pastor's wife. I remember one quirky moment during Holy Week: I had run out of Thin Mints and was on a personal mission to track some down—a rare reason to leave the house during lockdown. While I was on the phone with her sharing my "Thin Mint quest," she mentioned that Pastor Dawn was hosting a virtual foot washing.

That was the first time I tuned into any of Pastor Dawn's virtual services. I began to engage quietly at first, joining some Q+ Facebook groups where The Table's message resonated deeply with me. At that point, I didn't fully grasp what The

---

2. see footnote on page 189 for more information

Table was, but Pastor Dawn's presence and ministry kept surfacing in meaningful ways.

As time went on, Pastor Dawn's online sermons were reaching hundreds, even thousands. At one point, she commented on a post I shared in the ELCA Middle Tennessee Facebook group, thanking me for sharing her videos. I'll admit—it was a bit of a fanboy moment for me!

By 2021, The Table had left its previous space and relocated to the second floor of the downtown church I was attending. It had become my home congregation and I had become more actively involved. Pastor Dawn set up an office but I was honestly too intimidated to introduce myself. Eventually, the other pastor's wife intervened and facilitated our first meeting during a queer Mother's Day dinner The Table hosted for those who had experienced family or community estrangement. We officially met in the assembly room at that event.

I remember seeing Pastor Dawn's contact information circulating with an invitation that asked, "How can we support you?" or "How can we help you?" Despite my initial hesitation, I eventually reached out. On Easter Sunday 2021, I texted Pastor Dawn after worship, asking if she was offering any Easter services, assuming she might host something online. To my surprise, she proposed an in-person gathering. She posted an open invitation online, and soon we were worshiping together in the side chapel [which later became known as the Open Seating Chapel, a beautiful and welcoming space].

That Easter marked the beginning of my regular worship attendance at The Table. At my most consistent, I was there nearly every week. I maintained my primary membership at the host church but viewed The Table as both a necessary personal supplement to my faith journey and a ministry I needed to advocate for as a matter of justice. The Table did their best to ensure that any queer folks who needed a centering, inclusive space for faith could access it.

What was the condition of your faith prior to joining The Table?

I've always been a self-guided, self-driven learner. With ADHD "up the wazoo," learning has always happened for me in very specific, sometimes unconventional ways. For example, in elementary school, my ideal way to spend the day was imagining an ocean outside the classroom window and pretending I was swimming in it. I was perfectly content in that imaginary space.

It wasn't really until high school that something clicked. I started noticing the social benefits of academic success within my friend group, and that motivated me to pursue excellence. Not everyone has that kind of external motivator, but for me, it was important. I wanted to become a learned person, a scholar.

Getting into honors classes at my high school was difficult if you hadn't already been placed in advanced tracks back in elementary school or sent to special schools for the academically talented. I had to fight for it, lobbying, advocating, and working hard to make sure my performance data reflected what I knew I was capable of. Within a year, I went from taking math in the basement to being enrolled in honors classes.

My first honors teacher, Mary Beth Ellis, who was from Kentucky, talked to us about the idea of *seekers*. She explained that what makes an honors student isn't just grades, but a deep, self-directed desire to seek information. Seekers chart their own learning and don't wait for formal instruction. That idea resonated with me. I also remember reading about Benjamin Franklin, who was largely self-taught because he didn't receive formal education in the way we think of it today. He studied independently because he had access to information, and that shaped him profoundly. That model stuck with me.

So, even before The Table entered my life, I was already on a clear route of independent study, especially when it came to my faith. From early on, I recognized the need for a Q+ supplement to my spiritual life, because the anti-queer voices in the Church were so loud. Homophobia, like racism, is baked into so much of our culture, including church culture. It requires constant attention and counteraction.

Before I found The Table, I sought that supplement through resources like the Queer Theology Podcast[3] and the Deconstructionist Podcast[4]. I was also connecting with inclusive spaces like Trinity Lutheran on West 100th Street in New York[5], a Reconciling in Christ (RIC) congregation I watched online during the [COVID-19] pandemic. Then I found The Table, which not only provided spiritual learning but added a crucial layer of fellowship. That was something I hadn't really had before, in a Q+ faith space. So while my faith journey continues to grow richer and more scholarly, The Table remains a significant chapter in that story, both for the learning it offered and for the rare, vital fellowship it provided.

How would you describe your growth journey during your time with The Table?

(NOTE: Christopher's answer includes the 3R's woven all throughout)

About a year into attending The Table regularly, I launched *Queer Critical Faithful*[6] (QCF). The Table is an important part of that narrative. My learning arc has moved from private study and podcasts through The Table's community and the 3 R's (Reframe, Reform, Reclaim) and now into a public theology project. While there are some fellowship moments connected to Queer Critical Faithful, it's all digital, asynchronous. It's not the

---

3. https://www.queertheology.com/listen/
4. https://thedeconstructionists.org/
5. http://en.tlcofnyc.org/
6. For more information about Queer Critical Faithful visit https://www.instagram.com/queer.critical.faithful/

same as being together in person. That absence of live, embodied fellowship has been deeply felt.

As I reflect on how my faith has grown, I realize that much of what I now practice as a theological educator and liturgical content creator is directly rooted in the pedagogical foundation Pastor Dawn modeled. One of the most significant influences has been the way I approach serial sermonizing, sermon series, and liturgical series—and, more importantly, the narrative structures I create between the lectionary texts themselves. Pastor Dawn excelled at this. She recognized that the spiritual and theological lessons our community needed couldn't be contained within stand-alone sermons. They needed to be threaded across long stretches of time, building themes that allowed deep learning, reflection, and growth.

As educators know, true learning requires generalization. It requires the ability to take a concept beyond its original context and apply it elsewhere. It also requires the capacity to teach what has been learned. Pastor Dawn's mastery of liturgical teaching embedded both of those principles in her preaching. She wasn't just offering sermons. She was cultivating learners, teachers, and practitioners of progressive, embodied faith.

QCF is a direct product of that legacy. The project has only grown and now requires a significant amount of study. Study that wouldn't even be possible without the technology that helps me research and produce content. Even though AI assists with the heavy lifting, I still have to read, reflect, and study deeply. I'm grateful to say, the trajectory of my queer, reflective faith has remained steady. It keeps getting deeper, richer, and more complex.

My writing work at QCF follows the lectionary and demands a lot of theological engagement. For example, an ELCA Lutheran church in Sacramento shares every piece of content I produce. We also created a queer Christian content creator collective through my page's broadcast channel, where a handful of us—

like *Theology Queen from Connecticut*, who's leading the charge for drag and faith with over 7,000 followers—encourage and support one another. Yet, also true, and what's still missing since The Table closed, is the in-person spiritual fellowship. All of these themes point toward what I now call Embodied Faithfulness—a spirituality that not only reflects and learns but acts, resists, heals, and builds community.

As I recognized Year C [in the lectionary reading cycle] as a kind of capstone in this journey, I began to ask myself: If Year C is Embodied Faithfulness, what have Year A and Year B represented? When I reviewed my work from Year A, the answer became clear. That was the year I focused on confronting harmful texts and toxic theology—the spiritual cancer metastasizing within parts of the Christian tradition. My work that year was about neutralizing that harm.

I realized Year A was defined by what I call Deconstructing Faithfulness. Importantly, it's not faithfulness itself being deconstructed. Rather, it's a type of faithfulness that is so committed to spiritual integrity that it actively seeks out what is damaging the soul, and dismantles it. We aren't abandoning faithfulness. We are fostering a deconstructing faithfulness. That's the heart of *"Reframe,"* the first of the 3 R's Pastor Dawn taught us. Which led me to the next question: What, then, is Year B?

I have so many layered memories of my time at The Table—some joyful, some uncomfortable, all of them transformative. I remember the late-night work grind sessions, building our donor database and trying to wrangle people over the internet. It was chaotic and tiring at times, but those moments taught me how to organize in real time, how to communicate with clarity, and how to keep going when the work was messy. Those lessons directly shaped my ability to step into broader leadership. Honestly, I don't think I would've been able to organize the Downtown Churches Association if I hadn't first cut my teeth doing community work at The Table.

That season was also when I started exploring graphic design—just trying things, experimenting while helping out with social media. Because I was frequently posting, I began testing the platforms, pushing creative boundaries, and trying to find my visual language. But I quickly learned that there are spaces where experimentation is welcome, and others where intention and clarity matter more.

I recall one post where I'd outlined some older adults in rainbow colors from a social event. Looking back, it just didn't land well. It was awkward, not aesthetically sound, and distracted from the overall message. Pastor Dawn passed along some gentle feedback she'd received, and even though it wasn't critical in tone, I could tell she was worried about how I might take it. That moment stayed with me. Not just because of the post, but because it made me reflect on how I process feedback, and how important it is to move from defensiveness into openness.

At the same time, I was doing daily vulnerable Lenten reflections inspired by *Black Liturgies* (Cole Arthur Riley's project). Somewhere during that journey, the idea hit me: I needed a creative space of my own. That's how *Queer Critical Faithful* was born—out of Lent 2022, out of feedback, out of spiritual hunger. Having a space where I could explore design on my own terms gave me balance. It freed up my creativity so I could show up to church communications with focus and clarity, knowing the objective of the post, the audience and the outcome. QCF became the outlet where I could grow, stretch, and play, and that, in turn, strengthened the work I did for others.

One of the most intense learning experiences I had at The Table came during a moment of deep conflict. I'd gotten into a major disagreement with another member over a decision that had been made—something that was handled by the collective. It blew up. Pastor Dawn offered to mediate, and at first, I felt under attack. My emotions were high, and everything felt fragile.

But before we even sat down for mediation, I began reflecting. I noticed how I'd been triggered, and how my presence had triggered someone else. I could suddenly see something I hadn't wanted to see about myself. And that was profound. Sometimes we subconsciously avoid recognizing parts of ourselves that might challenge our self-image. But at The Table, surrounded by people who carried similar church traumas, I could see myself mirrored in others. It was humbling. And healing.

What shifted for me in that moment was the realization that equity required me to decenter myself. I was used to identifying with the marginalized, and in most ways, that was true. But in this particular dynamic, the power imbalance leaned in my favor. I had another spiritual home, another base church where I was fully connected. The other person relied on The Table for their primary spiritual care. That realization shaped how I showed up now. Not just in that conversation, but in life.

It was the first time I practiced radical equity in a way that wasn't just theoretical (*reforming*). It wasn't just "don't speak first" or "don't take up all the space." This was deeper. This was about listening with love and yielding ground when necessary. As a white man, I know that kind of self-awareness doesn't come naturally. But The Table gave me the conditions to learn it, practice it, and hold myself accountable to it.

Looking back, *reclaiming* those frustrating, awkward, emotional moments is where the biggest growth happened. The discomfort became sacred ground. And even now, I carry those lessons forward in every space I enter.

How did Pastor Dawn's leadership style differ from what you were used to or experienced with?

The first word that comes to mind is *openness*. Pastor Dawn leads with what I would call a beginner's mind. That is, an ability to meet each moment fresh, without forcing it into preconceived categories. She brings presence into every space she's in, and responds to whatever the present calls for. That's part of what makes her leadership feel so dynamic.

At The Table, this meant she was always willing to support the ideas, needs, and dreams of the community. If what we needed was a library, we built a library. If it was queer square dancing, she said, "Let's dance." Her leadership was deeply responsive, rooted in the real needs of people. And that made it not only powerful in person, but surprisingly powerful online. Even through a simple weekly livestream, her presence reached people across the country and beyond. But it wasn't just that people tuned in, it's that they reached out. People started writing to her, asking for help, seeking pastoral care. And what that shows is that people could sense, even through a screen, that her leadership was grounded in compassion, spiritual depth, and real-time receptivity.

The Table wasn't an easy community to lead. It was, in many ways, a Mötley Crüe of the religiously traumatized. People carried raw wounds, deep questions, and windows of tolerance that were often stretched thin. We were a group of people carrying a lot on our shoulders because of what the world had tried to take from us. That reality created moments of profound intensity. Pastor Dawn had to hold space not only for our healing, but also for our volatility—and she did so ethically, compassionately, and with as much equity as possible.

What impressed me most was her mindfulness. When situations became emotionally charged—and often, they did—she could take a step back, assess things without jumping to conclusions, and stay grounded in what was in front of her. She didn't lead from ego or assumption. She led with clarity, presence, and discernment.

There were times, I'll admit, when I wanted her to be bolder, especially when it came to standing up to Institutional structures. That seemed to be the one force that could dampen her otherwise fierce spirit. But now that I'm in significant leadership myself, serving as Council President at my own church, I have so much more empathy for what she was navigating. There's a weight that comes with spiritual leadership that's hard to understand until you're carrying it. And Institutions? They don't yield easily.

What's remarkable, though, is that even when Pastor Dawn faced setbacks or resistance, those moments became templates for our own growth. God used her life as a living curriculum. The things she wrestled with—starting a nonprofit, facing rejection, navigating systemic tension—those were the very things some of us would go on to experience. Her journey became a guidepost. When I traveled to Israel, I felt the echo of her spiritual wrestling. As I helped rebuild the Downtown Churches Association, I recognized how much I had learned from watching her lead The Table. It felt intentional. It was almost as if God had placed me under her care to prepare me. I can't say I've ever had that kind of relationship with a Sunday morning pastor.

Being part of a church community is like being in a relationship. Scripture uses that metaphor all the time. And, like any relationship, you start to realize what you need, and what you're capable of giving. At my Sunday morning congregation, I have space to lead. I get to steward history, maintain structure, and solve problems. All things I'm good at. I also have access to low-stakes fellowship, where connection doesn't always carry so much emotional or spiritual charge. At The Table, however, the fellowship was high-stakes. The learning was deep. The accountability was real. And the leadership was spiritual in a way I've rarely seen: vulnerable, powerful, and profoundly shaped by love. That's what makes Pastor Dawn's leadership unique. It's not just bold—it's deeply intentional, tender, and transformational. And through her ministry, so many of us learned not only how to follow Jesus more faithfully, but how to lead others with love, humility, and courage.

When I came I was _____ and when I left I was _____.

When I came to The Table, I was already on a fresh journey of healing and growth. But The Table was like God adding the fudge and the cherry on top of the bowl of ice cream. There was something about it that completed the journey.

There's a passage in Genesis when God speaks to Abraham and says, "Follow me and be blameless." But in Hebrew, the word often translated as *blameless* is *tamim*—which actually means whole, finished, complete. I think that's what The Table was for me: a *tamim* moment. After everything I'd walked through to that point, I joined The Table, and it made me whole.

Before I came back to church, I was in a really rough place. I mean, I was done. Done with life, done with faith, just…done. And yet, God wasn't done with me. If you had introduced me in 2025 to myself in 2017, I wouldn't have recognized who I had become. Sure, I'm still funny, still smart, still a little chaotic and inconsistent. On my best days I give everything I've got, and when I can't, well, it's average. But spiritually? The shift is night and day.

In college, my nickname was Pagan Chris. If you had told Pagan Chris in 2002 that he would one day help lead a queer church plant, or become the council president of one of Nashville's oldest downtown congregations, he would have laughed you out of the room. And probably stolen your drink. Emotionally, I'm still intense. But I've learned how to hold people with more intention. I don't just feel everything, I fight for clarity. I try to see others, not just react to them. The way I respond to heartbreak has changed, too. I've had relationships end in the past that left me paralyzed. But recently, when a relationship ended, I handled it with a level of spiritual maturity I didn't know I was capable of. I wept, I prayed, I sought God. And then I accepted what couldn't be changed and kept moving. That kind of resilience only came because of the spiritual transformation that happened at The Table.

Before The Table, I was a good writer. But after The Table, I became a published poet, a graphic designer, and the creator of over 1,000 unique pieces of queer religious content. I began experimenting with generative AI video, learning how to turn hundreds of tiny digital components into visual theology, as if each piece were a brushstroke on a sacred painting. That visual creativity was something I'd always longed to explore but never had the right space to nurture. And that's how I knew I was exactly where I needed to be: when parts of me that had been lying dormant finally began to blossom. The Table was the catalyst I didn't know I needed.

Sometimes we spend our lives knowing we are meant for more, but unsure how or when that "more" will finally emerge. And then God places us in the right space, with the right people, and something clicks. Everything we have been through starts to make sense, and new life begins. That's what The Table was for me. It was a space of resurrection because resurrection doesn't come without crucifixion. And The Table was a critical component of my ever-ongoing resurrection, my revitalization, and my return to wholeness.

When I left The Table, I was... resurrected. Not perfected. Not finished. But risen into newness. I left with vision, with calling, and with a creative fire that hadn't just been lit, it had been fed.

What is your greatest joy now?

One of the greatest joys and passions in my life now is Queer Critical Faithful. And the truth is, I don't think it could've ever come into being without The Table. When The Table closed, for a lot of people that was a hard stop. A painful period at the end of a beautiful sentence. But for me, QCF was already in motion. It had already become one of the greatest fruits of what I received during my time there. And that's a blessing I don't take lightly.

Is there any part of your story we did not talk about that you would like to share?

A Word Study in My Own Voice: *Tamim* and *Teleios*

There's a scripture in Genesis 17 where God says to Abraham, "Walk before me and be blameless." But the Hebrew word isn't really "blameless." It's *tamim* (תָּמִים). And *tamim* means complete. Whole. Sound. Not flawless. Finished.

When I think about my time at The Table, that's the word that keeps echoing. I came into the space already on a path of healing, already doing some of the internal work. But The Table —The Table was the place where the pieces started to come together. It was like everything I'd been moving through finally landed somewhere. That was my *tamim* moment.

And then, just like with Abraham, that *tamim* didn't happen first. It came after the call to walk. After the following. That's how it works. It's not 'be blameless and then follow.' It's follow, and through that, you become whole.

But wholeness didn't look like harmony. There were moments at The Table, hard ones, where I clashed with people. We had real conflict. I remember a particular disagreement that blew up, and for a while, it felt like we were completely broken. Like resolution wasn't even on the table. But then something happened. As I sat with the tension, I realized I could see myself in the other person's pain. I recognized their wounds. And I recognized the way my own actions mirrored things I wasn't ready to admit about myself. That kind of confrontation?

That's completion. Not because it felt good, but because it was real.

We talk sometimes about how God looks into the broken places in us, not the polished ones, not the staged ones, but the shattered spaces. And still, somehow God says: "You are whole." That's what *tamim* feels like. It's not neat. It's not finished in the way the world defines finished. But it's deeply true. So when I say that The Table made me whole, I'm not saying it fixed me. I'm saying it gave me people who reflected me. People who unknowingly showed me the parts of myself I couldn't or wouldn't see—and who loved me anyway, or challenged me anyway, or stayed anyway. That's wholeness.

In the New Testament, there's a word that picks up where *tamim* leaves off: *teleios* (τέλειος). It shows up when Jesus says, *"Be perfect, as your heavenly Parent is perfect."* (Matthew 5:48) And again, it's not about flawlessness. *Teleios* means full-grown. Mature. Reached toward completion. James says it like this: "Let perseverance finish its work so that you may be *teleios*; not lacking anything." (James 1:4) That perseverance? That was The Table.

Sitting in the conflict.

Owning the triggers.

Staying when it would've been easier to run.

Forgiving. Being forgiven.

Creating anyway. Loving anyway.

Teleios isn't a static end point. It's more like an asymptote. You're always moving toward it, getting closer, never fully arriving, but still becoming. That's where I am now. Still walking. Still working through it. Still learning to let myself be seen and still call myself whole. So yes, *tamim* and *teleios*. Wholeness and maturity. Brokenness and resurrection. All of it is still unfolding. And all of it is real.

What would you like to leave as a public witness for others who may read this?

My honest prayer is that every person who was part of The Table—whether one of the 4,000 followers online, the 30 core members around Nashville, or the 100 or so in the broader region—found something of The Table to keep alive in their lives. Something to carry forward. Maybe for you, it's not a public ministry or a social media page. Maybe it's a mindset. A language. A restored sense of belonging. A spark of creativity. A deeper commitment to justice. Or simply a clearer glimpse or deeper understanding of God.

Whatever it is, find that seed. The one The Table planted in you. Nourish it. Water it. Tend it. Watch it become something you could never have imagined. Because like Jesus said, *when a tree falls, it drops its seeds. And from that, a forest is born.* That's my hope for the legacy left by The Table. That's my prayer for every Beloved who passed through its doors, its comments, its livestreams, or its altar. That's what I want people to know about The Table. It wasn't the end, it was a beginning. And every Beloved who touched it carries a seed worth planting.

Let the forest grow.

Christopher's Afternote:

And still, I have to be honest. The way The Table was closed caused a lot of trauma. It caused me to question the ELCA in some real and painful ways. I know, denominationally, the ELCA is trying to address its overwhelming whiteness. I know it invests in marginalized ministries not just to perform the gospel, but because the Institution is actively trying to become what it should have been all along. But sometimes, the moves the Church makes feel hollow. The closing of The Table is one of those moments. It didn't feel like we were supported to thrive. It felt like we weren't profitable enough to justify the effort. And while there were definitely things that could have been done to sustain The Table, I don't think anyone was bold enough to actually try.

Yes, it would have required abandoning the fantasy that The Table would ever look like a middle-class church. You can't try to recruit marginalized communities and then punish them for not conforming to the dominant culture. We're not the dominant culture. That's the whole point.

So yes, there's been trauma. Relationships are strained. Being around each other sometimes feels like being around the pain itself. That's real. It's devastating.

And yet, my hope is still this: That one day we'll reach a place where we can be with each other again. Not just in memory, but in community. We all remember who we were when we were just seedlings in the garden. But I want to walk through the forest that The Table has left behind. And to see how tall we've grown, to see what beauty has taken root in our lives. That is my public witness. The Table was sacred. The pain is real. But the story is not finished.

Let the forest grow.

THE INTERN NOW
REVEREND WESLEY KING

"I know even those little changes made a huge difference in people's lives. I feel like the churchy people would have thought, 'I don't get it.' And I say, that is okay. Maybe it wasn't for you. But for the people we served, it was."

PASTOR'S PERSPECTIVE

It is hard to describe my journey with Wesley in a way that really does him the justice he deserves, and that we deserve together. I'll begin with this: He is a force to be reckoned with. At first glance one would be tempted to say something like 'what a charming young man.' After-all, his smile lights up a room and his energy is quite contagious. When he sings one would think the angels have gathered 'round the pearly gates for a sit-in. Yet, if you ask him, he's humble enough to say a simple 'thank you' and move on about it.

Prior to Wesley I had supervised a few Field Education students from a different seminary so I had a rough idea of how a year of internship could look. But I am not a cookie cutter supervisor and The Table was not a cookie cutter ministry. It was critical for me to do the leg work to find out why a person wanted to intern with us. All of the interns have been members of our LGBTQ+ community so that is not necessarily the drawing point, although, for Interns I believe it may have been. I was more concerned with the why than the what: let me review your Learning Goals and proposed outline for the academic year, then we'll talk.

Yes, I was protective of folks at The Table. Yes, I launched a very big protective umbrella over us—there are few who will do that kind of advocacy, including the Institutional Church. For folks who were often crawling in the door on bloody stumps, mostly caused by the Church herself, yes, I was protective. Wesley understood that. He neither took it for granted nor considered himself better off than any of us. At the beginning and end of each day, we were all queer folks in a queer ministry wading through religious derogation smack dab in the middle of the homo-trans-phobic Deep South. And in our state's capitol, to boot. Wesley took it all in stride and moved through it all with grace and candor.

I am honest enough to say I learned as much from him as he claims to have learned from me. That is the sign of strong leadership and humble people. One of my proudest moments was an invitation to speak at Wesley's ordination. I'll close with a snippet of that Commendation:

[T]hrough learning and growing, I knew the minute he started to play that music was his strength and ministry through music, in particular. Wesley said he wanted to challenge his growing edges; he wanted to preach and learn how to protest and learn how to rebuild. So we did that together for over a year. Lives have been changed for the better because of his time with us. Not only at The Table, also here in Tennessee and especially throughout the city [of Nashville]. Wesley's culminating project was in music. He helped us write a hymn. I am not a musician; it was one of the gifts God left out of my recipe, so I was very happy to be under Wesley's tutelage in that way.

He taught us a great deal: He taught us how to write theologically; how to think theologically; how to sing theologically. At The Table we are constantly pushing back and reframing scripture. So that we can see ourselves as queer folks represented. If you can't find yourself in the Word, you can't find yourself in the body of Christ. So we reframe and we reform the ways we think and the ways we inhabit our being, the ways we embrace our faith -- and then we go reclaim it! And we do it in tangible ways. And Wesley, you helped us to do that, you helped me to do that, and I believe that you learned also to do that -- in the pulpit, behind the keyboard, with the people in the sanctuary.

I have always encouraged Wesley to lean into his full authentic self. And just when you think you know the fullness of yourself, God will turn it up just a little bit. So, on that day when you ever feel fully capable and fully ready is the day that you should stop. Never, ever get comfortable. Not in the pulpit. This is a major responsibility and I know you know that because you practiced it so well. It is my joy and my honor to tell you that you are so, so ready to meet the world that God has for you to change.

This Commendation would not be complete if I did not send you off with our Sending Prayer. I'm going to ask you to stand. And friends, you need to understand this Sending Prayer is part of our reclaiming work that we do every Sunday night. We say these words over ourselves, out loud because we believe [them]. We trust and believe that when we say these words out loud, that God captures them and brings them into the center of God's heart. And they are shaken up and stirred up and given back to us in a refreshed faith. And that is what you need moving forward from today.

So Wesley, you are a blessing, you are not a burden. The world is a kinder and more wonderful place because you are in it. You are loved by God and cherished for who you are in your Creator's eyes. Now may you go in confidence knowing you are a unique and precious creation. Amen.

How did you find The Table and how did you find Pastor Dawn?

I heard and learned about Pastor Dawn through some of my Vanderbilt Divinity School connections. I had heard wonderful things and I knew that The Table was a new church.

I had been working in denominational ministry for New Church Ministry, the church planting arm of the Disciples of Christ. I was leaving another parish but I was in the middle of my MDiv[1] at Lexington Theological Seminary and I needed an internship site to continue my program.

I knew that I wanted a placement that was non-traditional in as many ways one can interpret *non-traditional*. Not so much the type of worship, more so like the fact that The Table was far and away a different kind of gathering space. They did not meet on Sunday mornings; when I began they were meeting in a regular room, not a church space. And the fact that their ministry focus was so vastly different from almost every other church I could think of in Nashville; they were serving people that nobody else was serving. And because of that, I sought out Pastor Dawn. And I was like, 'Hi, I need to do this internship. Do you think I could do it at The Table?' That is how that started.

[I asked Wesley to help me understand what he meant by 'a far and away different kind of gathering space'. He was gracious to expound:]

What I was interested in about The Table is that they were meeting the needs of queer people, LGBTQIA people; and that because of that, their ministry looked different. I mean, just the fact that they met on Sunday nights; because trans* folks felt a

---

1. MDiv stands for Masters of Divinity. It is a graduate level education in a seminary or divinity school and is often required in mainline denominations to pursue ordination as a pastor or deacon.

little safer (in regards to passing[2]) if they could come out at night. With their commute, the transit from getting from their house, their safe and comfortable zone, to this place.

That is just one example but there are so many examples of how this entire ministry was just different. Even amongst affirming churches, I did not see something that was queer centric. Whether it was intentional or not, it was heavily ministering to the trans community. And I just did not see that anywhere else in Nashville, that was appealing too.

It also felt like a ministry that met people at their most basic level of need. I think about the Community Hope Chest a lot. There were people grabbing stuff from there all the time. I saw many times where you had to provide support for some of our trans siblings who were experiencing homelessness, to coach them in survival. That is not always the easiest thing because sometimes they had to give up pieces of themselves just to be able to have a roof over their head. Just because we are in Tennessee.

[Wesley and I had a side conversation about some of the topics of conversation that I had with folks at the church. Topics ran from basic social skills, to safe sex, to deeply theological personal quandaries and religious trauma. Another pastor (or parishioner in general, or therapist even) may not think it to be pastoral to coach somebody on survival. I remember hearing that quite a bit—about the ways in which

---

2. In the transgender community, "passing" refers to gender presentation and involves expressing one's gender through clothing, mannerisms, and other social cues that align with their identified gender. In terms of social perception and safety, when a transgender person passes, others assume their gender without question. It can be important as it may reduce discrimination, improve self-esteem, and facilitate social integration. Passing is controversial in the trans* community in that some view it as a necessary step towards acceptance, while others criticize it as reinforcing gender stereotypes and pressure to conform. In general, it is a complex and personal experience. Not all transgender individuals desire or achieve passing, and it does not validate or invalidate their gender identity.

I counseled and conversations I had with folx. Sometimes we had to talk about safe sex and STDs: Just because you can't get pregnant, you still have to take care of your sexual health. I remember talking to one of my family members and they said, "You talk about that with your parishioners?" I said, "Yes! Because it matters and this is what pastoring this church is.]

The first time I walked into The Table there was a bowl of condoms. I mean, it was ministry like I had never seen it before. That was both appealing and why I wanted to intern there. It is so much of what I take with me now, that I've finished that internship, finished that degree and I am now out ministering in the world.

What was the condition of your faith prior to joining The Table?

I had reconciled a lot of the fundamentalism I grew up in. I had also reconciled a great deal of my own sexuality by the time I arrived at The Table. I think what grew out of the internship as far as my faith and spirituality goes, is just a deeper connection to justice. Because I saw it face-to-face here. There were many times that were really hard Sundays. Not that they were bad. Some of them were really good and hard at the same time.

I fondly remember one Sunday when one of our trans siblings reaffirmed their baptismal vows. Just seeing her standing up there, a trans woman coming out later in life, after serving her country, being a woman who the Church despised and disparaged—she stood up there and affirmed that she believes Jesus is the Christ and she wanted her new name, her chosen name, to reflect that baptismal vow—it was amazing.

Also, one time after completing my internship I came here on a Sunday night because I needed support. Someone told me about a sexual assault they had experienced that day. It was to be a hard Sunday. But, I knew that The Table was open and I knew you would be here, so I came. I needed it. It was a safe place for me. I didn't know what to do [and it didn't even happen to me] but I knew I could talk to you about it. So I came here and I did that.

Ministry was very blunt here. And blatant. Whereas at other churches you go, you sing songs, hear a sermon, it is great. Then you go home. It was just really raw and gritty here; really in your face, in ways that I had not experienced. It definitely was a place where your hands and feet got dirty and we were not afraid to get down in it because that is where the pain was and that is where transformation could happen.

I knew if I had gone to another church they would have let me preach. They would have let me preside. They would have let me do all those different things and that would have been fine. But I felt like I really got to experience ministry, like getting your hands and feet dirty, here. And I still got to preach and preside and do all those things, too. But I felt like this prepared me more. My preaching will get better as I get older and continue to do it; And presiding, the same.

Yet, being thrown into a ministry context like this, I think prepared me more than just being able to preach a lot, or to preside at the table, or pray a lot. I got to do that here too, sure, but just knowing the ways that The Table ministered to people in ways that I would not have even thought of...Like the condoms thing. Not that I had any issue with talking about safe sex but seeing it as ministry in motion[3] was unique. Seeing it

---

3. Regarding talk about sex, safe sex, etc. Our membership at The Table were all adult LGBTQ+ folk and our allies 18+. All conversation was consensual and sought out. No inappropriate talk took place; Although in a queer space "inappropriate" is a relative term. I would suspect conservative Christians would have been uncomfortable with the deep richness of our conversations. But as a practical theologian, I minister to my flock in ways that are real: real life issues and struggles. In real life, humans have sex. Therefore, safe sex is a topic I was willing to have with dignity and integrity intact.

here at the church in a way that says, in effect, if we are going to talk about it or experience it, then, here is access to live it.

All of the ministry at The Table was similar: If we are going to talk about poverty, if we are going to talk about the trans* community needing a safe place to try on clothes, or find clothes —And our unhoused neighbors—there were just so many different ways that I *lived* ministry instead of just talking about it like we did at school.

[It occurred to me to provide some further context, details that Wesley and I spoke of often during our Supervision sessions: As a seminarian, we are taught in the academy how to think critically. But thinking critically and living critically are very different exposures. And it is a very different skillset. It can be really difficult to learn to live it critically, but it is ever so important and necessary to meet people where they are in life.

Prior to ministry I worked for the Department of Emergency Management and we did safety drills, tornado drills and natural disaster drills. Drill, drill, drill so, theoretically, you are "ready" because you are practicing. But in a church context, particularly in a place like The Table, we do not have the benefit of drills. This is real life, in real time, with real people. There is no time for a do-over. You are just in it, and sometimes you are in it before you realize you are in it.

Being prepared in the academy to think critically is a fantastic skill set to have but sometimes, when the rubber meets the road, you have to choose whether or not you are going to get your hands and feet dirty. In a place where you may not even know what the hell you are doing, or if you belong there. Neither of us are trans* and I verbalized that often: 'I'm not transgender, so I do not actually know what it feels like. I can only do the best I can do to serve your needs, right here, as you share it with me.' It presented a ministry challenge that was always 'to the best of our ability,' whatever our ability was at that moment. And by God's great grace, and honest sharing by our trans siblings about what they needed, between the three of us: you (or) me, God and the person, we got the need met.]

I just thought of two other things about how The Table prepared me: I feel like I have used my MDiv and my time at The Table (experience, skills, and anything that I learned there) in my nonprofit work, too, with Nashville in Harmony (NiH)[4], more so than I have in ministry contexts since I left The Table. Nashville In Harmony is an LGBTQ+ musical arts organization filled with people from all backgrounds. People have called me when their parent has died by suicide. They have called me when they want to talk about their own spiritual upbringing and how to reconcile those things. There are so many things that I learned at The Table and in my MDiv time that I use at Nashville in Harmony. I don't know that I would have been as prepared to handle those things had I gone to an internship in a traditional setting.

The other thing is, I loved the creativity at The Table. Because it was a new church start, we were able to try things. If they worked, great, we kept doing them. If they did not, it was a good idea, and that is okay. That is not necessarily something seminaries teach. It was an amazing experience to be able to try new things. That was exciting. People have thoughts about creativity. Some think, creativity is just 'these things.' This person is creative, this person is not. My time at The Table was a good example of *no, everybody can be creative*. Let's try it and let's not only do it just for shits and giggles but for the fact that creativity is a spiritual gift that everybody can exercise.

[With regard to creativity and what it can look like in ministry: As an LGBTQ+ person of faith, one of the things non-affirming spaces try

---

4. Nashville in Harmony (NiH) was founded in 2004 as Tennessee's first musical arts organization specifically created for people of all sexual orientations, gender identities, gender expressions, and their allies. With a mission of using music to build community and create social change, NiH brings people together within both the LGBTQIA+ community and the community at large. Find out more information by visiting their website at https://www.nashvillein harmony.org/

to take from us, in addition to our sacredness and our right to be a spiritual person, it tries to take from us any vestige of joy we find through creative arts, or through creative thinking, or through creative dreaming, even. Non-affirming spaces are death dealing not life-giving. And so to be able to come to a place like The Table where we did our best, and still do our best [through projects like this book] to be a place of life-giving—a place of transformation—even if you walked in the door with death in your hands, we could find a resurrection moment in it. And do it collectively.]

Describe the lifecycle of the 3 R's in your faith journey.

That framework—I gobbled it up. I still use it today. The first example I thought of was my MDiv Capstone. I wrote on music, hymnody, spirituality and religiosity. I used the framework of the 3 R's to look at why we sing what we sing; the entire project was through the lens of those 3 R's. So, it not only informed my spirituality, it informed my academia.

[*I asked Wesley if he would say that the 3R's became a critical analysis tool for him?*]

Yes, absolutely. And it is a framework that I have utilized in other ministry contexts since leaving The Table and my internship. And it is one of those things that other people have since heard about and now use. It is a tool, the seeds keep getting planted and growing in other places. So I would say it is something that definitely informed me as a pedagogical tool, as a critical analysis, and then also as a framework for ministry; for scripture and exegesis both then and now. I still use it.

Something else, too. You used the 3 R's when sermonizing. But we also used it when we were talking about music. We used it in ministry in general but we also used it in the liturgy at The Table. By the end of my time there it was in sections of *reframe, reform, reclaim*. There were pieces that fit under specific sections such that it was not only an exegetical tool, it was not just a musical tool, but it was the liturgy. It was the work of the people, so that it was lived. It was not only a heady thing, we got to live into it.

[With regard to using the 3 R's as a pedagogical tool: Speaking as a preacher, it is really important to me to give people more options to think about. I do not fancy telling people what to think, or how to think. But I love giving people lots and lots of options for things to think about. However, they have to be useful, they have to be practical. I have often said that if you leave my presence after hearing a sermon and you cannot put into practice what you heard me say five minutes ago, I have not made myself relevant enough.

You have got to be able to use it. Because it is a really hard world out there. It should be a very short walk from the pulpit to the pew. At least that is my opinion. The pulpit is not a place that has a pretty little pearly gate around it. It should be, as you [Wesley] said earlier, foundational and messy. It should be able to get down and dirty and give people tools to live by in the real world. Because faith is real. I call it embodied faith, and it is real. People have to be able to hold on to it—and some of us, hold on for dear life—grasping as tight as we can.]

How did Pastor Dawn's leadership style differ from what you were used to or experienced with?

(NOTE: I encouraged Wesley to expand his answer as wide as he could since he was with us as an intern first, and later as a guest preacher, ministry colleague, and community partner through NiH.)

I left the church I had been working at for almost five years because the new minister was not collaborative or inquisitive. As an example, in the way we [denominationally] practice communion, people would come up to the table. Some people could not get up to it because of the steps, so it was not accessible to everybody. We moved it down to the floor. The new minister moved it back immediately. With that, there did not seem to be a question of how best to serve.

My experience with your leadership style began with you asking me *what do you need and how can I help?* And that is something that you asked everybody. But as the Intern, it was something you asked me, and I think that that leadership style allowed me to…I think I could have come here and just preached and prayed and whatever. But I think that leadership style allowed me to explore so much more of ministry here at The Table. That is something I want to take with me into my work, too. That question immediately gets to the heart of what people need and desire. It is not instructive, it feels collaborative. It feels like *shared ministry.*

I just cannot imagine people not responding well to that kind of approach.

How would you describe your growth journey during your time with The Table?

(NOTE: combines question about experiences that helped your thinking and BE-ing)

Well, that Parker Palmer book[5]. The one that I initially hated, and you kept telling me 'just lean in'. That is definitely one example of my growth. Mainly because I am someone who likes to plan and a lot of that book is *give up your plans.* That did not comfort me, it challenged me. Which it was supposed to. As I have come to understand ministry a little bit better, that book is more of a *be prepared* because who knows where God might lead you, where the Spirit might lead you. So I appreciate that book a lot more than when you first gave it to me. We did a lot together.

---

5. Palmer, Parker J., *Let Your Life Speak: Listening for the Voice of Vocation.* 1999. John Wiley & Sons Inc.

But I think that was one of the only things that you said, like, this is homework. You have to do this. Everything else was optional and collaborative. And I am glad that you made it mandatory because I would have not done it. [We enjoyed a good time of laughter just now!]

The other standout is the moment the trans woman reaffirmed her baptismal vows, that was a really big moment for me. I think it was the audacity of this person, who has been so hurt by this Institution, to be like, "Nope, I'm doing this." That was really impactful. And there are so many more. My Capstone was a huge one. Being able to lead people through that process. Again, back to the 3 R's.

Would you like to share more about that?

A graduation requirement to complete my MDiv from LTS included a Capstone project. Something that would benefit the local church, the church I was serving, in particular. As I mentioned earlier, the project centered on hymnody and music because of my music background. I used the 3 R's to reframe, reform and reclaim LGBTQ+ spirituality and identity within hymnody, within music.

Looking at some hymns we knew, we *reframed* some of the words that gave us some pause; whether it was around theology we no longer subscribed to, or that we learned in the faith of our upbringing. We reframed them into words and sentences that felt more life-giving for us now. We also went through and *reformed* language in those hymns that did not provide the amount of inclusivity that we know God to be. I learned a great deal here [at The Table] about expansive language for God. I had heard about it but seeing it in practice was a big thing. We analyzed hymns and changed pronouns or descriptors of/for God that did not speak to us, in an attempt to bring our whole selves to the practice [of worship through music].

Finally, we practiced *reclaiming* by writing our own hymn. We used our own words, our own values, taken from the *Mission* and *Vision Statements* of The Table and used the meter that the hymn provided to create a hymn that was fully ours; that conveyed who we are as people, using language that includes all of us, not just traditional he/him pronouns. We used theological words that specifically reflect our lived experience; something we could claim as our own. It became a reclamation of our own spirituality. Ultimately, we wrote it and then sang it as a part of that reclamation process. (NOTE: The hymn is included in Part IV, *LifeNotes.*)

[It was certainly a life-giving experience. So much so, that a few months after the hymn and your project were completed, we had Bishop's Convocation (a denominational retreat for clergy). I had given a listen to the bishop and he chose to use it during worship. It was a very proud moment for me; and for you because I held you in my heart as we were singing. Everyone had a printed copy so they could read the lyrics. It was a gift to behold, to be sure. Scripture says 'you will know them by their fruit'—that is some good fruit for a synod full of pastors, 95% of whom are straight people, the vast majority of whom are white men. It was a beautiful moment.]

When I came I was _____ and when I left I was _____.

When I came, I was ready to change it up. When I left, I was the one who was changed.

What is your greatest joy now?

Not that this is anything new but there has been a renewed spirit behind the attacks on the transgender community. I think about the ways The Table was a safe haven for trans folks. I remember there was a time when someone said The Table is a 'trans church.' We said no, it was not a trans church in that all people were welcome there. But I do think it is a testament to how safe transgender people felt there. I am really proud and it brings me a lot of joy that The Table was able to be that for people. Because we know, you and I know, that the State of Tennessee can be very tumultuous for trans folks. With this new Administration and especially in Nashville, TN, it has been like this for a while but now there is a renewed attack on the trans community. Just knowing that that is something The Table provided, and that I was a very small part of it, that is a proud moment. It brings me a lot of joy.

Is there any part of your story we did not talk about that you would like to share?

I am so grateful for the ways you and The Table supported me during my Internship time. I mean The Table being a sponsor for my musical (*Ten Year*, King and Heinz, Nashville, TN) so that that story could be told; The Table being a place where I could do my Capstone project. The Table gifting me the commentary set; You and others from the church showing up to my wedding; You participating in my ordination service. I mean and not just you, several folks from The Table attended. So, just the ways that The Table supported me and has continued to in different ways, both metaphorically and literal tangible ways.

What would you like to leave as a public witness for others who may read this?

I think that we think we have an idea of where the Spirit is moving or what the Spirit is doing. We often dismiss things and say [or think] 'no, that can't be what the Spirit is up to.' I think from my time at The Table there are so many examples of things that happened that so many people would have dismissed. I felt, saw, and knew without the shadow of a doubt, that the Spirit was moving in it. I think too many people, Christians namely, would have dismissed it. We like to box God in as much as we can. But there were so many times that I was sure *this is the Spirit moving so vividly, so clearly.*

People need to remember that. A lot of what I just said is meant for *already churchy* people. I think about the really Orthodox folks, who would have not really understood why we did the Lord's Prayer the way we did. Yet, I know even those little changes made a huge difference in people's lives. I feel like the *churchy* folks would have thought, why change it? There were so many changes like that. I feel like the *churchy* people would have thought, 'I don't get it.' And I say, that is okay. Maybe it wasn't for you. But for the people we served, it was.

Pastor's Afternote:
Wesley is right about one thing for sure, many of the churchy people, including synodical staff did not understand why we did ministry the way we did. They rarely, if at all, took the time to engage or learn. Maybe it wasn't for them. I say, it could have been. Wesley is absolutely correct when he said, 'but for the people we served, it was.' It was indeed.

Eucharist looked very different at The Table. First, our Lord's Prayer was modified so that all people could access grace, forgiveness and communion with God. Not all people see G-d as a boy, a girl, a man, a woman, or a physical being. For some, religious trauma has kept them from the altar. For others, clergy abuse (often sexual) has kept them from being able to see G-d as a male-identified figure. And still, for others who were abandoned by their birth mother on the sole basis of their gender identity or sexual orientation, G-d could also not be approached as a loving female mother figure. For that reason, we reframed our language toward a more appropriate, useful, honorable and desired orientation to approach the Eucharist.

Second, because we streamed live on camera, and only some folks/x were "out" while at worship service, I came out of the chancel and served communion individually at the pews. As a trauma informed pastor, the care I provided had a very different approach from the traditional. I took the onus upon myself to incorporate trauma informed care into every aspect of pastoring. For me, and for our membership, it was critical to rebuilding a healthy faith relationship with the Divine.

One of my favorite prayers will always be "A Contemporary Lord's Prayer @ The Table"[6]

Our Mother, Our Father, Our Parent in heaven:
May your holy name be honored; may your Kingdom come;
may your will be done on earth as it is in heaven.
Give us today the food we need.
Forgive us the wrongs we have done,
as we forgive the wrongs that others have done to us.
Do not bring us to hard testing, but keep us safe from the
 Evil One.
Yours is the Kingdom, power and glory, now and forever.
 Amen.

— ADAPTED FROM GOOD NEWS TRANSLATION
(GNT), MATTHEW 6:9-13

---

6. Pastor Dawn wrote this version of the Lord's Prayer as a trauma-informed prayer and to be accessible by all.

LANCE'S SEARCH FOR WELCOME

"My growth can be measured by my increased level of spiritual peace. Finding refuge at The Table caused me to breathe more deeply the fresh air of faith."

PASTOR'S PERSPECTIVE

Each week thousands of people watched our worship service online. We streamed live in real time Sunday evenings with as many online as were in person in the sanctuary. What happened from the Monday morning after, through the Saturday evening post, I do not have an answer for. But God.

When I was inviting guest writers for the earlier chapters, it occurred to me that this book would be incomplete without the voice of our dedicated online community. One person in particular came to my mind. I invited Lance to reflect on the same questions that others, including myself, expressed our thoughts on.

Lance's story is important because it shows his dedication to his lived experience. He may be states away, yet his pain, his joy, his commitment to finding a life giving path through a journey that can be isolating at times—it is as if he is right around the corner. Intimate details of the joy and sorrow of LGBTQ+ life in a church setting are interwoven because we are, afterall, family in a unique way. Lance, I'm so grateful you honored yourself and your faith by joining us in this story.

How did you find The Table and how did you find Pastor Dawn?

I found The Table and Pastor Dawn in an online search following a troubling sermon preached at my lifelong church. My search was an attempt to find local "welcoming" [city,state] churches. However, the results also included other geographical areas. The information regarding Pastor Dawn in Tennessee intrigued me, and I was immediately drawn to her persona and purpose.

What was the condition of your faith prior to joining The Table?

The condition of my faith was rather weak, wounded, and very much fueled by frustration rather than inspiration. Created by God exactly as I was intended to be—yet my pastor was touting the "love the sinner and not the sin" theory. Categorized amongst rapists, murderers, drug dealers, and pedophiles, I was feeling more and more incapable of tolerating the toxicity.

How would you describe your growth journey during your time with The Table?

My growth can be measured by my increased level of spiritual peace. Finding refuge at The Table caused me to breathe more deeply the fresh air of faith. I'm free to be myself when Pastor Dawn preaches. There is no fear. Only freedom.

Describe the life cycle of the 3 R's in your faith journey.

The reframing, reforming, and reclaiming produce a magnificent recipe for the very real and raw reinvention of my faith system. To reframe what was inaccurately taught gives me proper license to adjust the falsehoods and eradicate the prejudices. In reforming the damaging lessons, my control is restored and no longer am I manipulated by the guise of God per other's ignorance. Finally, via the reclaiming of my faith, I'm confident and calm. God is in the mix!

How did Pastor Dawn's leadership style differ from what you were used to or experienced with?

Having been merely an online congregant, I can only imagine how satisfying it would have been to participate in actual outreach efforts. Pastor Dawn's efforts to respond to my inquiries, thoughts, and input surely made my path better and better. I'd be honored to emulate her version of outreach. Pastor Dawn's brand of leadership represents a refreshingly approachable theme. She is the grassroots of grace. There's a delightful difference in her vibe. Peers should take note.

[I will note, we have only met online and via email for the entirety of our pastoral relationship. This is one person I am blessed to know, as a piece of peace.]

When I came I was _____ and when I left I was _____.

When I came to The Table, I was despaired and when I left I was empowered.

What is your greatest joy now?

My greatest joy has its foundation in my newfound connection with Pastor Dawn's path. I will have faith in her faith when mine may occasionally falter.

What would you like to leave as a public witness for others who may read this?

Jesus loved all. No exceptions. Find your God within yourself. Nature nurtures. Go forth.

Pastor's Afternote:
Because we were in different time zones, I recall always being watchful to not begin, or ring the [Tibetan] bell before I saw you online. I am grateful for your contribution, Lance; for your willingness to stay in touch and for your continued hope and belief in yourself and God. You are a living example of why this work matters. Be healthy, be whole, be blessed.

PART III
MAKING HISTORY

Olivia's Legacy
Ginger Widens WELCA
Veronika's New Stage

OLIVIA'S LEGACY

"Pastor Dawn never once asked us to change to fit into a church. She changed the church to fit us."

PASTOR'S PERSPECTIVE

I knew when I first met Oliva it would be a dynamic relationship. Her career as a steam plant operator was fascinating to me, in and of itself. I had never known a woman to have such a trailblazing career. In the early years of The Table, Olivia was an instrumental person in helping us launch some of our initial ministries, namely the Transgender Support Group and Community Hope Chest.

One of my funniest memories happened at a Mother's Day brunch event. I was on the dumbwaiter balancing a rolly cart filled with food, drinks, and decorations. After reading all the safety signs, I made sure to close the door tightly behind me. The danger emblems reminded me of an amusement park when the loud speaker belts out, "keep your arms and legs inside the ride at all times." So, with myself and my rolly cart securely loaded, I hit the red button.

If you have never been on a dumbwaiter before, you may not know that the red button is the safety alarm, not the down handle. With a fright and a scream, I panicked. Frozen in my fear, all I could think to do was yell out Olivia's name. And very loudly! She came quickly and calmly. And with a giant smile, she reached in and pressed the red button to turn off the alarm. Then, with a gentle smile [and nothing else] she pressed the down handle. I had a very safe six foot descent after that.

That was the beginning of the many times Olivia would not cease to impress me. We have talked together and counseled on so many life issues, they truly are too numerous to count. The reality for adults who transition later in life is that they have a whole host of life experiences under their belts: family, marriage, divorce, parenting, career, financial stability and the like. Transition often takes all of it away, causing otherwise well-adjusted and fully independent adults to have to revisit earlier life stages, as they are forced to rebuild their lives.

Olivia is a strong, empowered, and vibrant personality. She commands the space she is in. She fills it with light and positivity; it is hardly possible to diminish the energy (and who would want to?). I'm so grateful for the opportunities I have had to minister to and with Olivia; I am convinced we have changed the face of Nashville, TN for the better, despite our continued legislative challenges here.

Thank you, Olivia for believing in yourself, for taking risks, for pressing onward, for running for office, and for your public servant leadership. We are all better for your presence in our city.

NOTE: Like two others, Olivia wrote most of her own chapter, focusing on what was lasting and impactful for her and her journey. Not all of the interview questions were answered, and I tried to fit those that were in where they seemed most appropriate. Others, you can imagine, have answers that live on very vibrantly in Olivia's everyday life.

How did you find The Table and how did you find Pastor Dawn?

Initially, I met Pastor Dawn as she was marching down Broadway at the Pride Parade. It wasn't long after that I found myself connected to the humble beginnings of a ministry that changed the face of "church" for the LGBTQ+ community, at least in Tennessee.

When I look back on the story of The Table, it feels like remembering the blooming of something sacred—something that the world desperately needed but didn't yet know how to ask for. I was there at the beginning, when it was just a dream carried inside the heart of one extraordinary woman: Pastor Dawn Bennett.

How did Pastor Dawn's leadership style differ from what you were used to or experienced with?

The Table wasn't built with grand cathedrals or endless committees. It was built with open hands, open hearts, and a fierce, unshakable belief that everyone deserves a seat at God's table. Pastor Dawn had a vision of a community where the outcast would not just be welcomed, but celebrated. A community where the LGBTQIA+ community—and especially the transgender community—could not only survive but thrive.

I was excited to join in this new ministry, not just because I loved the idea, but because I could feel the pull of something deeper—something life-changing. I knew, even before we gathered for the first time, that The Table would be holy ground.

From our very first conversations, it was clear that The Table would be different. Pastor Dawn didn't want to create just another space where marginalized people had to sit quietly at the back. She wanted to flip the entire structure. She wanted the marginalized to be the heartbeat, the very center of everything.

Describe the lifecycle of the 3R's in your faith journey.

In those early days, we often met just to dream together—to imagine what could be. We didn't have all the answers. But what we had was enough: we had love, and we had hope. And in the middle of a world that often felt cold and closed-off, that was revolutionary.

When the COVID-19 pandemic hit and the world came to a grinding halt, The Table refused to close its arms. If anything, we opened them wider. Virtual gatherings became our lifeline. Across Zoom calls and chat boxes, we found ways to reach out, to connect, to love. And out of that chaos, we birthed one of the most beautiful traditions I've ever had the privilege of witnessing and being part of.

How would you describe your growth journey during your time with The Table?

Community outreach was a big, big part of life at The Table. We launched monthly online gatherings where we took part in sacred storytelling. These were not typical church services. They were sanctuaries within a sanctuary—safe, sacred spaces where healing could begin. The first meeting of each month was dedicated to storytelling where a different trans person was invited to share their journey. We created a space where, perhaps for the first time in our lives, we could tell our full story without fear—without judgment. There was something absolutely breathtaking about those nights.

I can still see it: a trans woman sitting before us, hands trembling slightly, tears brimming in her eyes, taking a deep, steadying breath—and then opening her heart. She spoke about growing up feeling different. About hiding her true self to survive. About losing family, jobs, sometimes even homes. About nights spent praying to a God she was told would never love her.

Over time hope began to sprout up. Stories were shared about the first time someone looked in the mirror and recognized herself— About the day she realized she was worthy of love, belonging, and joy— About finding The Table. Each story was a sacred offering, a light breaking through the darkness. And as we listened—through laughter, through tears—you could almost feel the bricks of shame, fear, and loneliness falling away. We could feel the community forming, heartbeat to heartbeat.

For every new person who sat in that circle, who once thought they were alone in their pain, it was like watching a new star be born. I'll never forget the looks on people's faces— the quiet relief, the radiant pride, the dawning realization: I am not alone.

Our second gathering of the month was designed as a tool for growth. Special guests and speakers were invited, often professionals who could give our community the knowledge, resources, and strength they needed to live boldly and safely. We had police officers who spoke about personal safety and how to advocate for ourselves if confronted with discrimination or danger. We had grief counselors who walked us through the complicated landscape of loss—loss of family, loss of identity, loss of safety—and how to heal from it. We even had sessions on legal rights: how to create a will, how to assign a power of attorney, how to protect our life and dignity in a world that often overlooked us.

Every gathering, every conversation, was an act of love. A reminder that being trans is not just about surviving—it's about living fully, thriving, and building a future.

We were building a community one story, one lesson, one heart at a time.

Is there something you learned or experienced during your time at The Table that helped your thinking and BE-ing?

One day during one of our idea sessions, I mentioned something that had been tugging at my heart: a dream of creating a closet—a place where trans folks could come and find clothes, shoes, wigs, breast forms, packers, and whatever else they needed to step into the world as their truest selves. Pastor Dawn didn't even blink. "Yes," she said. "Let's do it."

Not long after that, we found ourselves at a department store which was going out of business. I still laugh remembering the sight of the two of us rolling giant metal clothing racks through the parking lot, negotiating the best deals we could for The Table. We must have looked like we were setting up our own department store. We were—but it wasn't for profit. It was for hope. Those racks went into a little space we lovingly named the Community Hope Chest. In no time, shelves were filled with donations—beautiful clothes, shoes, accessories—items chosen with love and care.

I'll never forget the first time I saw a trans woman walk in, pick up a dress, try it on, and look at herself in the mirror. At first, she barely recognized herself. She adjusted the wig, smoothed the skirt, and hesitated. And then—a smile. A real, radiant, bone-deep smile. For the first time, she saw herself the way God made her: Beautiful. Worthy. Whole. There were so many moments like that. First smiles. First tears of joy. First time feeling seen.

None of this would have been possible without Pastor Dawn. She didn't just lead The Table. She poured her entire heart, soul, and spirit into it. She showed up for every single person. She hugged. She prayed. She laughed. She cried alongside us. She gave her heart away over and over again—and somehow, it only seemed to grow bigger every time. Pastor Dawn never once asked us to change to fit into a church. She changed the church to fit us. She reimagined what faith could look like—and in doing so, she made space for countless people to come back to God after years of exile. She was—and still is—the heartbeat of The Table.

When I came I was _____ and when I left I was _____.

[I answered this as the pastor who has watched Olivia grow and blossom over these past five years. I have watched, encouraged, kept company and witnessed as she has navigated some of the biggest hurdles of her adult life; All while she maintained her poise, her integrity, and her inner beauty.

When Oliva came she was a somewhat timid, hopeful, and self-motivated lady; and when she left, she had fulfilled her dream and passion to become the first openly transgender person in the State of Tennessee to be elected to public office. And to that I say, well done, good and faithful servant.]

What is your greatest joy now?

When I made the heartbreaking decision to step away from my leadership role to run for public office, it was done purely out of love and protection. I feared that my public campaign could bring dangerous attention to our vulnerable members. I could not allow my own ambitions to risk the safety and privacy of those who trusted us.

Even though I stepped back, The Table has never left my heart. I continued to attend worship online on Sunday nights. We also formed a new type of relationship: that of community partners and advocates. Pastor Dawn's guidance, love, and fierce truth-telling still echo inside me every day. The community we built still fuels my steps. The hope we planted still blooms in every speech I give, every law I fight for, every door I walk through proudly as my full, authentic self.

What would you like to leave as a public witness for others who may read this?

The Table was not just a place. It was a movement. It is a living testimony to what happens when love wins. It is proof that no matter who you are, no matter where you've been, no matter how many times the world has tried to break you—you still belong. You still have a seat at The Table.

GINGER WIDENS WELCA

"When I came I didn't know who I was, I was in search of an identity. When I left, my identity was firmly in place because I realized I had a purpose."

PASTOR'S PERSPECTIVE

Some stories I hadn't heard from start to current. I was called to build a church. I began that task formally in January, 2020. Nobody, certainly not me, saw a pandemic coming. Nobody, certainly not me, understood the magnitude of both the church and the pandemic. Ginger's story has been an inspiration from the moment I met her. She has 'smiling eyes' and her energy is palpable. Even before I met her in person, I knew I was in good company.

I remember meeting Ginger for the first time. We had been hosting monthly online transgender support groups. As pastor it was my role to open the online room. My intention was to turn the host duty over since I did not feel like I belonged in the room. I am not trans*, a detail I found myself repeating for over a year. For many reasons, the group asked me to stay and facilitate the online gatherings. With hesitancy I *agreed but only under the condition that I could sign off at the top of the hour, to leave the rest of the time for a closed group discussion. (Because if you don't know, there are things that need to be discussed outside the earshot of cisgender folks, pastor or not. I knew that, or at least hoped that.)*

Almost immediately the group grew from four or five to almost fifteen. Each gathering opened with the lighting of a candle (to usher in the presence of Spirit) and a round of check-ins: Highs, lows, and a gratitude. An important detail I learned very early on was that if there is one thing transgender folks lack the most, it is the opportunity of taking up personal space in the world. That became the gatherings purpose—to take up as much space talking about your life as you chose to.

I provided members with a template for writing their story, a guide basically, since nobody had experience writing from that lens and their vulnerability was palpable. Still, it was important and necessary work that centered the 3R's (not even fully developed back then). Each month we sat intently listening to the finer details of the storyteller's life. Suffice it to say, Ginger has had a compelling life thus far. I did not know her prior to her transition, and I wonder how different today's personality style is from her former life. I know, in this life, Ginger is a powerhouse of a woman. She is vibrant and funny. She does not know a stranger. And if you need someone to lift the spirits in a room, Ginger is your gal.

To say I am proud of her is an understatement. To say I am grateful for her participation in this project, likewise. And for the record, she also now has a polished workshop she presents around the country. What you need to know about Ginger is that she IS changing the face of WELCA[1], one synod assembly at a time. That is quite a feat. Believe

---

1. Women of the Evangelical Lutheran Church in America (WELCA) is a national 501(c)3 and aligned with the ELCA Lutheran Church. For more information visit https://www.womenoftheelca.org/

me when I tell you, it is quite a feat, indeed. Also, I love that Ginger calls me "PD."*

How did you find The Table and how did you find Pastor Dawn?

I am a woman of transgender experience, who recently came out. I like to say I'm a woman who was raised as a man and learning to be a lady. And that's kind of the start of my journey. I questioned my gender identity for years. Actually, ever since I was a child because there were some issues there. I didn't always fit in, I never really had friends. I relate better to women than I do to guys. I didn't inherently have male privilege, I could tell that from the guys I worked with. It was a kind of weird thing.

I was married for forty-six years. My wife developed a very rare, very severe non-covid viral infection that got into her brain. As a consequence of the damage, she lived the last few years of her life in a nursing home. At the time of her passing, I had already been dressing as female socially[2]. My wife and I had a do-not-ask-do-not-tell arrangement so she didn't know much. She didn't like it. Being transgender, at our age, was not something we witnessed.

When my wife passed away, I made the decision that life is short and I really needed to be me, Ginger. That's when I made the decision to come out fully. I was born in 1947. The generation who didn't talk about stuff like this. So, I embarked on a journey of curiosity: how do I interact with society now? I'm

---

2. This sentence describes "social transition," the process where a person begins to live and express their gender identity in ways that reflect their gender identity, rather than their sex assigned at birth.

suddenly single; I'm now suddenly a different gender, I am known in my church as Gary and they didn't have any idea about me [Ginger]. There are generalizations in all of our transition stories but it is important to say that no one's story is exactly the same. My story is definitely not a straight line to transition (pun intended).

I went to GriefShare[3] because I had heard that was one of the best ways to start processing the feeling of my wife's passing. As the last session drew near, they talked about acceptance. Part of the acceptance of death is that you have to reinvent yourself. I said, "Oh, my God." I had a feeling, a really weird feeling. There were six ladies in the class, me being one of them (at the time I was living as Gary). I made a comment, "Ladies, I need to tell you something..." I could tell they were puzzled by their facial expressions and in large part my confession of being transgender was not a good thing. (I might add that now, two of those people have become some of my best friends at church.) The next week, I came to GriefShare as Ginger. Jaws dropped, but I was welcomed and it felt really good.

A month later, I made the decision that my church needed to know. I had been discussing things with my pastor for well over a year. He knew what was happening and about the path I was on. I had been going to Trinity Lutheran for almost 20 years, and now I was changing my path. The day had come. I got out of my truck, in a dress, as Ginger, and I shook for about five minutes. Then, I made the decision to go in. I got a lot of looks; I got a couple *hate* looks. But I also got a lot of thumbs ups. At the end of service a lot of people said, *wow that's a journey*. From then on, I started living as me.

I don't remember if I got referred to The Table by my pastor

---

3. GriefShare. https://www.griefshare.org. Information provided by the Author for information purposes only. Not an endorsement of services or organization.

or by another member who was the youth minister. We were all sister churches of The Table. Meeting you [Pastor Dawn] was quite an experience for me and I didn't know what to expect. You and I got to talking and you welcomed me into the family and said, "Be you. We are different here. We are not traditional." I loved hearing that since I've never been a traditional, religious person. My parents didn't raise me in the church.

My Dad said he *had* to go to church and he hated it. So when he got back from the military in World War II, we only went on certain Holy Days. I have gone from neutral, to atheist, to agnostic, back to atheist, back to kind of believing, but I've never been "religious." And I will admit that even today, I am not a religious person. I believe in God. I believe in God as the energy of the Universe; as a Force, not as a grumpy old man who smites everybody who pisses him off. I believe in God as the Force that makes the Universe tick around. Likewise, the Bible is a history document; written and translated by men with varying biases and agendas. It frames the social context of how society works and it is also contextual, you can't pick and choose.

I couldn't go to The Table very often because it is a one-hour drive each way so I went when I had the chance, and most of the time I attended virtually online. I felt comfortable at The Table, I felt like I was with family. I didn't know where I was going, being a new widow, not sure of what kind of religion I'm looking at, what I feel, what I want to do. I just wanted some guidance.

You called me one day and invited me to go to the Southeastern Synod Women's Convention. Everyone in our group of women was either, transgender, lesbian or bisexual and you said it was going to be a fun trip. I think you knew I was a little bit nervous. I was actually beyond nervous, I was terrified and shaking, going into the conference with a bunch of cisgender, hetero-normative women. The wonderful thing is, I was so welcomed. The group of women I was seated with that day and throughout the weekend would say, "God loves everybody and I'm glad you came with The Table because we want to welcome everybody." That was the key to The Table, for me, it was the full inclusion.

I can still remember one particular night, the night of the convention dinner. I wanted to look really nice so I dressed up. I came down and you and a couple other ladies looked at me and said, "Wow! You look really nice." You called me a Fashionista. *[Dawn: I did, indeed!]* That to me, is inclusion. That told me right there, I was with family. That is how my journey started with The Table. I'm still not comfortable. I'm still a woman and I'm still learning.

What was the condition of your faith prior to joining The Table?

[I had to provide some additional commentary here because Ginger so honestly offered up that she is not a religious person. I don't consider myself a religious person either. I am a very devout person. There is an ocean of difference between the two, at least for me. What I will say, for clarity, is that The Table, in terms of a religious Church institution / organization, really was quite an anomaly. For most folks who were members, the condition of their spirit was something to be gently tended to and cared for. As the pastor, it was a poignant part of my ministry oath.]

I do not think I had a condition per se. I never really believed. I went to church with my wife because she did believe. I sang and did *churchy* things but I did not participate. Coming to The Table, I didn't know what the heck was going on and why God did what He did to me. But as we walked through the journey together, I started believing more and more that the church *is a community* and that God had a purpose for me. It's fair to say, my faith went from ehhhh, very weak at best, to *'wow! community is important and church is one way to be a part of that community.'*

How would you describe your growth journey during your time with The Table?
&
Describe the lifecycle of the 3 R's in your faith journey.

NOTE: Ginger and I entered this part of our chat in such a way that it was next to impossible to keep the cadence of previous chapters. What you will read below is our live discussion which weaved together a few questions. As often happens, most especially with older adults who have been married, raised families and had a few careers, life is a bit less linear and a lot more cyclical. We do not live in a vacuum and neither do our life experiences. For older adults like Ginger and me, it may be helpful to learn to appreciate this because life does make some definite changes, and not all of our changes are isolated or integratable. Neither are they all pleasant, or lifegiving. In the end, generally, they are all interwoven and useful, however. Ginger and I veered off the path a few times but I hope you agree that it was worth it and to keep our chat honest.

Ginger:

Reframing, for me, was defining what God meant to me, and where do I go with that. Again, not because of the biblical standpoint but just *Why me, God?* as a transgender person, who lost her wife. As my journey progressed and as I became more comfortable with who I am, we (PD and me) started talking about Women of ELCA (WELCA) and how to make that more active. As both the process and my journey continued to develop, I became more and more interested.

One of the key events was a phone call I received a couple years after I transitioned, from the synodical WELCA board:

"Ginger, we've been talking among the Board and we really like you! You're a really nice person. We think you'd be a perfect fit for the Churchwide[4] Women of the ELCA." I've never been involved in church activities, I would avoid them with a heartbeat except for at The Table when I helped with dinners and events. I asked to think about it a little bit.

I decided I needed to talk to another pastor. I talked with my pastor at Trinity, I talked with you and I wanted to talk with another local female pastor to get her feedback. Here's where it gets funny, maybe by God's joking. I had been working on the application for the nomination process, on my phone not on my computer, when she returned my call. We talked for a few minutes when I got another phone call which turned out to be spam. Now, when spam comes in we all hit the big red hang up button. Turns out that day, the hang up button was also on top of the submit button on the nomination application; Alas, my application was on its way! Like I said, maybe God's joking. It turns out, I met all the requirements. A month later, at the assembly in Phoenix, AZ, I was elected to become the first transgender woman of the Churchwide Board of the Women of the ELCA. That's God saying, "Hey, I've got a plan for you." And it all started with The Table. Now my faith has grown, my activity has grown, I have become much more of an activist. I'm enjoying every second of it.

Dawn:

Community is so important. It reminds me of a lyric that says, 'you never know what you've got till it's gone.' Community is almost priceless and sometimes we don't realize the value it plays in our lives

---

4. Point of clarity: WELCA Chapters happen on the local and synodical level. At the national denominational level it is referred to as Churchwide.

until you turn around and it isn't there. Sometimes it causes a reset altogether.

I can see how you've pruned and morphed from being a non-believer to a Believer, in the ebb and flow of not being a religious person, yet being a spiritual person. When I look at you, I can see God's countenance on your face because you have what we call 'smiling eyes.' I don't know if anybody has told you that before. What it means, in spiritual terms, is that God's face shines through you. It's quite a blessing; So it is not at all a surprise to me that the ladies on the Women's board saw that in you. And, for what it's worth, you did not look terrified at the conference. Perhaps it is that coming out or transitioning later in life has some unique perks after all.

Ginger:

I am not the same person I was growing up. I considered myself a nerd. I did not talk to people. As I reflect back over the last couple of years, I have changed 180° in my approach to life and the way I react and respond to people. Now you cannot shut me up whereas before you couldn't get me to talk, even though I had forty plus years as a Division Quality Manager and responsibility for six plants internationally. I've dealt with all kinds of people, all kinds of scenarios, and honestly, being a trans woman would not have worked in many of them. Many of the plants were culturally leaning and male privilege is a real thing; transgender women lose just as much as every other woman does. Suffice it to say, life now, as I live and know it, has become my *reclaim*. I have flipped myself totally. And I'm happier. And I think it shows.

Dawn:

It absolutely shows! It shows by the glow on your face. [you can hear Ginger laughing exuberantly in the background.] That is quite a testament. I also hope it's not lost on you, because it's not lost on me, that God allowed your career to flourish the way that it did so that you had more tools in your social tool bag when it came time to transition. Interestingly, in managing all of those people, all of those plants, you learned a lot of conflict management skills. You learned how to read the room, not only for people but also for safety—and a whole bunch of societal elements that—in the queer community—we are often on high alert about. I think the older we are when we come out or when we transition, we don't necessarily realize that we're using those early life skills and how helpful they are.

Ginger agreed with me and we went on to discuss the heartache we feel on behalf of younger queer[5] and transgender folks, most especially teens and young adults. We talked about the reality that they don't yet have the life skills to battle societal ills and dangers. We discussed that these skills are not "trans life skills," they're not "bi life skills," they're not "queer people life skills." They are people-in-general life skills. Skills like social graces, how to be in public, how to be in private, how to read rooms and situations for safety and other realities. Life skills are not a respecter of persons but the ways in which we carry ourselves in public—as queer people—requires an additional skill set. In earlier decades code switching[6] was necessary. I asked Ginger what she thought about it and if she finds that she herself code switches. True confession, I, Dawn, definitely code switch for a variety of reasons, my personal safety being paramount. And then there is my truth: I am a bisexual, female pastor serving in the Deep South which is a mind-bender for a lot of folks.

---

5. Ginger prefers to use the term "queer" in lieu of "LGBTQIA+" because it is easier for her to say.
6. "Code switching" refers to LGBTQ+ individuals changing their behavior patterns, speech, language, or gender presentation to avoid being stereotyped or treated differently due to their sexual orientation or gender identity. Code-switching is a default safety behavior to avoid or minimize discrimination.

Dawn:

Ginger, do you find that you code switch now or do you always present fully as Ginger?

Ginger:

At this stage, I'm almost having a hard time relating to Gary. Gary has become almost a different personality. I will say, I am much more aware of my surroundings. Last year I took a trip to Pennsylvania and I stopped at a rest area. It was not quite late evening, still dusk. As I got out of the car, I suddenly realized *I'm a woman, it's dark, I'm in a public place but it is remote.* All of a sudden, my head was on a swivel. So, yes I am learning new skill sets that I did not have before. But I'm also saying *hey, I can cope.* I may not have any testosterone left in me anymore, but I did then. And mentally I have all of the conditioning as having been raised in the male world, so I have the insight and the foresight.

How did Pastor Dawn's leadership style differ from what you were used to or experienced with?

One of things I really like about your leadership style is that you are non-traditional. You lead as if to say, 'let's get everybody involved.' 'let's think outside the box,' 'how can we make people comfortable?' 'how can we change the vibe?' It was an interesting learning experience. The leadership style had to differ based on the context. It wasn't always easy but I do think it was necessary, looking back on it. Your leadership also differs from my other pastor in that he has to be aware of the entire congregation. We have a lot of older folks and sometimes they tend to lean a bit more conservatively. So he's walking on eggshells in terms of what he can say and how heavily he can promote the queer community. Even still, he also draws a line in the sand and [essentially] says *everybody is everybody. All means all!*

The older folks are learning they have to accept people as they are. We now have myself as a transgender woman and I'm fully accepted. I have friends that I go out for lunch with every Sunday, including the pastor's mother. We have a mixed family that is black and white and the kids are a mixture of orientations and identities, and everyone is accepted. So that's a different style. His is more laid back, more let it build; You are more into the face. For me, both are great.

How would you describe your growth journey during your time with The Table?

There is so much. We had become a family. What is bubbling up for me in this moment happened toward the end. It was our final worship service together, in fact. There was a core group of us, who, even though we were not best friends, per se, we were friends. We all had a sense of purpose. When the hammer dropped [referring to our sudden and unexpected closure] and we were suddenly violated with the news that The Table was being shut down, unceremoniously in our opinion, we united.

The sense of belonging when that happened, was kind of amazing. We all popped on to our emails to the Bishop and to the Synod, about our objections. I was the one who vocalized it, in his face; and I got a lot of support afterwards from everybody. We were totally in support of you. This was the wrong thing to do. We had a mission. We had a community that served our purpose, that fed our soul; we had a huge online presence, several hundred, I believe. Our sense of community was strong, we were a cohesive group. We believed in the mission. We believed that the queer community needs special handling. We are fragile; we are marginalized; we are [told we are] the pariahs of society. At the end of the day the gays, lesbians and bi folks are pretty much accepted by society.[7] The transgender folks, not so much. So it felt good to me to have that sense of community. It was palpable.

I think one of the things The Table did well is strike a balance between the online family and the in person family. We were all together as a family in many instances. We went to dinner together, we volunteered together, we laughed and cried together. We partied together and supported one another through all kinds of ups and downs. That's what family does. Family is not always the group of people you are born into, it is who shows up for you on a daily basis.

When I came I was _____ and when I left I was _____.

When I came I didn't know who I was, I was in search of an identity. When I left my identity was firmly in place because I realized I had a purpose. Which in my case is to be an activist for the transgender community. Finding my purpose has spurred me on to create my workshop which now has been attended by a couple hundred people. My workshop has evolved, like my faith and like my activity. I went from *I did not know what was going on* to *I'm comfortable with who I am*. And a lot of that is because of The Table, and helping me to become who I am.

---

7. At the time of this writing, The Trump Administration has stripped DEI and all evidence of LGBTQ+ citizenry from all governmental websites. Any state or federal agency who receives federal funds has been forced to comply with this executive order; any institution who receives federal education funds has been also forced to comply. The Trump Administration has done its best to erase transgender and bisexual identities from the United States of America. The expectation is that it will continue in this fashion of erasing identities until all that remains is cisgender, heterosexual people. Given this was Ginger's interview, I did not interject this information into our conversation. However, it bears recording, as it is horrifically relevant in 2025.

What is your greatest joy now?

My greatest personal joy is just being me. It also brings me joy to see somebody's light bulb turn on when I explain to them what the Trans* Community is.

[I couldn't help but to get a bit giddy the moment those words crossed Ginger's lips. I had to interject: I mentioned your countenance and your 'smiling eyes,' you have a light within you. As soon as you said 'watching someone's light bulb turn on' I thought, 'that is it! That is what I see!' Ginger agreed.]

Is there any part of your story we did not talk about that you would like to share?

In part, I helped revitalize the transgender support group here in Nashville (a secular, social group, not part of The Table). As we shifted from the old Tennessee Vals[8], we reframed and repurposed to the Middle Tennessee Transgender Alliance. I was the Vice Chair. It was fun to help get that going again. I've since stepped back as we are trying to bring new leadership in. Ever since I first started going to The Table, I've had a Tuesday night Zoom meeting to provide transgender support. People come in and we talk, and we've helped people grow. It's called Ginger's Speakeasy.

What would you like to leave as a public witness for others who may read this?

The Table provided a sense of community; a sense of welcome; a sense of involvement that I didn't have before its

---

8. Tennessee Vals was a private support group for transgender folks/x in Middle Tennessee. The group has been renamed Middle Tennessee Transgender Alliance. Find them on Facebook for more information.

existence. So in many ways, I was able to pick up a sense of purpose. Learning about scripture in more modern Community terms was key. It was important to be able to understand and reinterpret things and see life in ways that make it easier to digest what they were talking about 4,000 years ago. And to have new insights to say, oh, this is different now. I think that my biggest takeaway is that I came. And in coming, I walked away with a better feeling about who I am. And a better feeling for what God means to me, which is not traditional; which is beautiful because I think God appreciates not being traditional. We have been trying to make God traditional for eons and it has never worked.

VERONIKA'S NEW STAGE

"I think my greatest joy is knowing that I can do it. I can be behind a pulpit, in heels or not, and still be effective... I am a more satisfied person knowing that they are full of shit."

PASTOR'S PERSPECTIVE

For me, Steve Raimo [aka Veronika Electronika, aka Sister Reya Sunshine] is a trifecta friend. We have been together in such a variety of spaces doing a variety of advocacy and ministry things, it is like trying to pick just one ice cream flavor—when anyone who knows me knows, they are all my favorite.

In 2021, when Governor Bill Lee began his derogation of LGBTQ+ life [in general] which seeped in and out of the state capitol, I knew I needed to kick my public theologian presence into action. Tennessee had become known as the Slate of Hate, leading the U.S. in anti-LGBT legislation. Not even children were safe. Discrimination has been legalized under Lee's Administration, using "religious exemption" as a legitimate reason to deny someone damn near everything. Naturally, because "the Bible says." I thought, okay, well, I too can claim "reli-

gious exemption" and put my faith into action by countering the Lee Administration with a scriptural defense that stood on its own solid footing.

In the few short years following, as if legalizing discrimination against LGBTQ+ children and adults were not enough, the Lee Administration turned its fist toward Drag Culture. Although later deemed unconstitutional (as if discrimination was ever constitutional?) the TN Drag Ban caused a big raucous and hate toward our community took an even stronger turn upward. All in the name of protecting 'what the Bible says.' (As if!)

Just as I had no invitation to the House floor, politicians had no invitation to my pulpit. But Queens did. I began a preaching series called Drag Me to the Pulpit. I sought out Drag Queens who were actively practicing their faith and their craft. I decided we would not be silenced, nor would I allow our queer community to crumble under the discriminatory bills and laws flying through our Legislature; at least not without trying to provide a safe haven and an affirming word of unconditional love—Jesus style.

Over the course of a few years, I aimed to have a Queen in the pulpit quarterly, Veronika was a popular return. She was local and folks loved her. She has a style and vibe all her own. She knows the Gospel and how to tell it in a way that catches your attention and lets you know beyond any doubt, Jesus is real and he loves you.

Steve, Reya and Veronika, I am blessed and thankful to know you.

How did you find The Table and how did you find Pastor Dawn?

I believe I met Pastor Dawn at a Music City Sisters[1] event. I'm

---

1. *Music City Sisters of Perpetual Indulgence* is an order of 21st Century Queer Nuns dedicated to the promulgation of universal joy and the expiation of stig-

pretty sure that's how it came about. It was Sister Rose E. Thorns elevation project, the prom[2] for LGBTQ+ students. That is likely where we first met. At the end of the day it does not really matter where we met, what matters is that it occurred. *(Dawn: And this, dear readers, is why you will come to love, love, love Veronika's candid personality.)*

And how I found The Table was, I think, just by getting to know you. I had been working at an LGBT affirming church years ago and was looking for another church home. I had been intrigued by going to a few different ones but they never quite jived. When I learned about The Table I thought, *'Oh, I can jive with this.'* Then I met you and we jived and the rest just kind of melded together.

[*Like many of the relationships I had as pastor of The Table, I was able to intricately weave my ministry and my community organizing together in a way that flowed rather fluidly, such that in many spaces the worship portion of The Table was smaller than the community advocacy portion. At the end of the day, they all fed off each other.*]

In contrast to many other organizations, a lot of the people who were involved with The Table were very community active people. A lot of "churchy people" are just "churchy people." So I think that was a little bit different about what we had going on. But several of the folks in leadership at The Table were also involved in other community groups.

It was very reminiscent of *"old school church"* whereas people from the community went to church. It was not just people from church who went to church. So it was a faith-based community gathering. That would be a good way to describe what The

---

matic guilt. They work to raise money for AIDS charities, fight for queer rights and visibility, and provide safer sex outreach. For more information visit their website https://www.musiccitysisters.com/

2. Twice a year The Table hosted a spring prom and winter formal for LGBTQ+ high school students. We partnered with MCSPI and PFLAG Nashville (https://www.pflagnashville.org)

Table was to me. It had a town hall community feel to it, yet faith-based; where ideas were discussed and emotions were allowed to exist while still focusing on spiritual growth and communication. It was a church on paper but it was so much more. It was so much more than a C-H-U-R-C-H.

What was the condition of your faith prior to joining The Table?

That question is almost like the condition of a used car. You need to know the condition of something in order to place value on it. But, I wonder, if something is in a bad condition is it worth less? I think when you are talking about faith, it can be misconstrued and can be used devisively. If we unpack it a bit though it can be answered subjectively, as if to ask *what is the condition of this old car*? Well, it has a patina. It has lived. It has the original paint. It has the original wheels. Is it in the best shape? No, it is sixty years old. Or you can say, what is the condition of this used box of tissues? Well, the paper is ripped; it is empty; its condition is poor. It has no value.

Looking at the vintage car, what is the condition? It has been loved. It has been used. It has been street driven. But it builds value, it builds a patina. So, you can look at it in any sort of way. What was the condition of my faith? Lived in; Tried and tested. Yet, it is road worthy. It has a couple dings; a couple rocks have hit the windshield. Have I needed to change the tires on occasion? Yeah. Have I had to fill it with gas regularly? Yeah. Because you have to feed the car. Even if it is a vintage car, if you want to drive it daily, you still have to take care of it.

I have had the benefit of never being uprooted. I look at faith like a tree, it will always be stronger if it is never disturbed. When a tree is transplanted it always takes a long time to reestablish itself. I look at faith like the roots of a tree, it is really not easy to move an established tree. Many people who grew up in churches had roots in that church setting, but when they *came out* or *transitioned* [or got married or divorced or moved] it is like somebody came and scooped up that tree and moved it, either by force or they moved it voluntarily. When it comes time to replant it someplace else, it can be very shaky and one has to pay very close attention and nurse that new spot. I was introduced to Christianity early, I was raised a non-practicing Catholic. I did the bare minimum: christening at birth; first communion in third grade; confirmation in seventh grade and that was it as far as a church journey in Roman Catholicism.

When I met my first boyfriend in high school, his family was Southern and he was a born-again Christian. I did not know what that meant. I did not know there was a difference between being a "Christian" and being a Catholic[3]. I always assumed *Jesus followers* were 'Jesus followers across the board.' So when I first learned what being a born again Christian was, a relationship that is not with a priest or a nun or a bishop or a pope. It was more of a personal relationship with Christ. I have never heard a Catholic talk about their personal relationship with Christ. I am sure they do but that is not a conversation that I have had.

I learned at my boyfriend's church it was more of a relationship with Jesus; that God can speak to you directly. It was the Reformation all over again, but personally. I now had answers to many questions I had for many years as a Catholic. I also did not have a home church, so my initial interaction with Christianity was personal. I was baptized in a creek in Pennsylvania and

---

3. For clarity, there is no difference between being "Christian" and being "Catholic." Catholicism is the original Christian Church, as in Rome. However, especially in the Deep South, there is a surprisingly pervasive view that Catholics are not Christians. It is quite rife indeed, and very incorrect. Also, since this was Veronika's interview, I did not interject that correction. I leave it here for readers.

shortly thereafter I moved to Nashville to pursue a career in Christian music.

That was the first time I made sure that my sexual orientation came into the conversation with regard to a church setting. I wanted to be an honest Christian, so I said, "Listen before you dunk me in this tank, I'm a gay man and I'm always going to be gay man and that's part of my faith, it's part of my DNA, it's part of my journey. Before you dunk me, I need to make sure that you are cool with that. Because I'm not being baptized in a lie. I'm not repenting for that." They assured me that everybody's journey is everybody's journey and they were not there to judge anybody. They acknowledged that I was there to accept the Lord into my life and this baptism was a public witness of that.

So, getting back, I think my stability and my faith is what it is because my faith was never shaken in that way; where I was told that I was operating incorrectly. I was never told by the church that I was lying or that I was deviant. I never belonged to a church body that told me that, nor did my family. Whereas many of my brothers and sisters at The Table had come from backgrounds where they had been shaken; they had been uplifted, or unrooted, or transplanted. So when they were planted back in their faith at The Table, it was a nice feeling [I'm assuming] for them to know they were in a safer garden. I think when The Table ended, again it was traumatic because they had already been through the trauma of being uprooted once and now we had to go through it again.

That process is very traumatic and it is not always successful. To answer the question as it's written, *what was the condition of my faith prior to joining The Table?* It was road weary but still ticking. The maintenance record was clean.

How would you describe your growth journey during your time with The Table?

There has to be two sides to this question because Veronika very rarely is the one sitting on the couch studying for what will be spoken about at the service. Veronika gets dressed and shows up, Steve gets to do all the work, for the most part. Having said that, I have always been an off-the-cuff speaker whether in preaching, when I was an Associate Pastor, in Drag entertainment or if I am an emcee at an event.

I have always felt that way in my Christian faith as well. I trust in the Lord to give me what I need to know, in the moment. Yet, what preparing for *Drag Me to the Pulpit*[4] allowed me to experience was the discipline of working through, "no, I really need to know what you're going to talk about and you need to write it out. You need to send it to me 2 weeks in advance." That blew my mind...I thought, I have no idea. It is very possible I will talk about *this*, and send the email. For sure that was part of the "tightening" of my faith. That was more along the lines of the logistics and preparation to be in a pulpit where you are addressing other people publicly in a way that is not a Drag performance. I am not lip syncing a sermon. That was a big part of how I grew during my time at The Table.

I also learned how to read the room differently. I do many different types of speaking engagements: I emcee shows, I do

---

4. In response to Gov. Bill Lee and the TN Legislature's brutal attempt to weaponize religious freedom and undermine sacred scripture by passing anti-LGBT and anti-Trans legislation, under the guise of protecting children and families and allowing one to invoke religious exemption, I also used this privilege to counter the hate speech and attacks on our queer community. I developed a preaching series I called Drag Me to the Pulpit where I invited Drag Queens who have previous pastoral and/or preaching experience, or who are active people of faith, to come and preach on biblical scripture. Veronika Electronika was a frequent guest preacher at The Table.

Drag Story Hour[5]; I speak at public gatherings and political events; or I am at a bedside talking with somebody. I have had to learn how to nuance what I say depending on where I am. I can deliver the same "message" in many different ways depending on who is listening to me. Sometimes I am intimidated when I am asked to speak at a particular place because I often feel like I am the least experienced person in the room, in regards to what the group of people do.

I was asked to speak at a convention of social studies teachers one year talking about the Drag Ban. It was strange because they were career educators. I wondered, what in the world am I doing here? Then I realized, people want to know about your personal experience. My time at The Table allowed me to hone that skill.

Still I speak in the moment. No, I will not have a written sermon, it is just not going to happen. You are lucky if I do not paraphrase the scripture that I am about to read. I will never win an award for most eloquent preacher because I have learned to trust my feelings of empathy, and to read the room, and to look into the eyes of people who are listening to me. And I would like to think that one of the spiritual gifts I have is to be able to feel the energies of the people who are in the room with me. I have learned to listen to myself too and realize when I am not jiving with what I am about to say—to decide on the fly, that, no this is not the message the room needs to hear right now. For sure though, my experience with The Table has allowed me to hone in on many of those things. I would not be at the place I am had I not had those pulpit experiences.

[I had to reflect on Veronika's words here because I watched her many times—maybe with a nod and wink out of the corner of her eye,

---

5. *Drag Story Hour* is a national and global nonprofit. Drag Story Hour celebrates storytelling through the dynamic art of drag performance. For more information visit https://www.dragstoryhour.org/

at me—I watched the spirit move through her (in a similar way that you read about Wesley having seen the spirit move in his experiences with ministry at The Table). I preach and teach often about embodied faith. If we cannot personally engage with what we are doing or saying there is a serious chance that what we are doing or saying will not land in our spirit. Yes, there is something to be said about rote prayer, discipline, intercessory prayer, and the work of the Spirit among us that perhaps we are not as aware of. And yet, to be connected to the 'still small voice inside' is to be in full communion with our Maker, in the moment, in real time.

As it relates to Veronika's time in the pulpit, I have watched people come to life [so to speak, spiritually] at the very sight of her speak and preach the Word, while in Drag. Her ability to reframe and reform her talking points, while reading the room, is evidence of two things: 1) Steve being connected to his Lord, in his spirit, prior to donning Veronika's dress and makeup and, 2) Steve's willingness to be used by the Spirit in a way that fulfills the reason Veronika is in the pulpit to begin with.

Veronika had a knack for speaking truth to power, diffusing theological understandings that have done great harm to our LGBTQ+ community. Her approach landed in a way that was both palatable and compassionate, with a side of humor. I really appreciate that because, particularly in the Deep South, and particularly for many folks at the Table, the hell-fire and brimstone preaching is what scared and damaged a lot of people in their religious life.

So being able to adjust on the fly is a spiritual gift, yes I do believe that, as I also experience it. Yet, it is also a gift not everybody has. It is not a gift that an insecure somebody-in-a-pulpit would often take. Speaking truth to power, speaking about the Gospel—on the fly—is a courageous step because once it comes out your mouth, you cannot take it back.]

[Steve] Right. And you can cause a lot of hurt. You can do it wrong. I try to put the sentences that are about to come out of my mouth through my brain at least twice when I am able to. If it is a *statement* I really try to think about it, especially when I am working with a group of people who experience a, b or c, [a) a plethora of spiritual abuses by family, friends and pastors; b) any of the many diverse orientation and gender identities community folks live; or c) a person who really feels 'they know better']. I often will try to filter [not filter to strain out things but to process, to make sure I am using the best words possible] and also to not trigger people. Also to make sure that I am being honest with myself and I am not just giving word juice.

[Word juice. I have never heard that description before. But s/he makes a valid point. Wouldn't we all be better off for this practice, both in and out of the pulpit!]

Describe the lifecycle of the 3 R's in your faith journey.

I have to go to the root of the question. When we are talking about *reframe, reform* and *reclaim*, you have to start with something first. So birth. Who are you born as? Who are you born with? Who are you born for? Who are you? We need to ask all of this because you cannot be *reborn* if you were never born. That has to be part of the communication.

When I talk about rebirth, or 'born again' is the term, I think you still have to pay homage to the person who you were when you were born. What were the highlights? What were the flaws? What needed to be fixed? What were the things that were missing? What were the things that were beautiful? What things were wonderful? Things that you wanted to share. All of those things need to come into context because the whole point of being a *born again Christian* is to leave behind the sins of the former you; that you have now accepted Jesus Christ as your Lord and Savior...ba ba ba...all the bumper stickers. *(Welcome to the...side of humor!)* I think that in order to respect the *rebirth* we still need to acknowledge the birth.

When I encountered Christianity, I wanted purpose. I

wanted to understand why I mattered. I felt like becoming a Christian allowed me that opportunity. I accepted that I mattered because I was worth the sacrifice of this God. Otherwise, I am just going through life feeling like I am only worthy for myself, or until I find somebody else who feels like I am worthy too. I think faith, based in a religious relationship, allows you to understand the concept of sacrifice. It allows you the concept of changing what your birth meant.

Reframe, to me, is the ability to create structure and to be able to say '*I am now part of this church body. I have some roots here and I can stretch out a canvas on this. I can create something new because the framework is here.*'

To *reform* is to really allow yourself to be in the mingle of the room. To reform yourself is to give body, literal body, to your faith. You are allowed to mix and mingle, and you are allowed to be confident on your Christian legs. It would be very difficult to do that successfully as somebody in the pulpit, or even just as a member of a church, if you do not feel confident that you have got some good sea legs under you. To *reform* that is to sure it up.

To *reclaim* is to feel value in what you already feel is going pretty good. And to reclaim part of who you were in your birth, before your rebirth. Even though you may not have been the ultimate version of you, there were still good qualities there. So you can reclaim some of those qualities. When you are *born again* it is not a clean slate. Many people say that it is. To me, it is not. To me, it is a refined slate. So, you kind of dusted off the extra pieces and you can use what you have been through as part of the character of who you will become.

[I did not say it at the time, but now that I have typed this out, I have to confess to you, dear Veronika and dear reader, that for me, this is the best description of what a 'born again Christian' can be. For me, your words do God, Jesus and the Spirit sincere justice.]

How did Pastor Dawn's leadership style differ from what you were used to or experienced with?

I appreciated your leadership because you were a *leader*; you were not a phone-in. That is what primarily comes to mind. My experiences with church leadership in the past were limited. Still, I do not know if I heard you say "no" very often; or, *that is not a good idea*; or, *I do not think we should do that*. I have heard you exercise caution; and I have heard you say, *let us pray about it*; or, *what do you think if we did this*. And I appreciate that. I think that is important as a church leader.

I hate *"churchy"* things. You often enjoyed engaging in the art of education as a church leader. And especially as a…mentor… that is a good word. I found that my time with *Drag Me to the Pulpit* was very much, to me, a mentorship. I never felt like I was less than or pupilish. It was more of a camaraderie. I felt that often. I think that sometimes that is lacking in many areas of leadership, whether it is church work or personal life; so I always appreciated that. Also, you allowed me lots of wingspace to flutter how I needed to, because you knew what you were getting into when you asked. [laughing] Like, what you print in that bulletin may or may not be what I actually talk about. I never felt inhibited, even though I was asked to prepare weeks ahead of time.

There were so many things along those lines. Also, I always felt appreciated. It was a very humbling experience for me. I appreciated the style of leadership at The Table, both from you and Wesley in regards to music, and your Tech person too, are all people in leadership positions. If you even wanted to include the bishop and the other people, how they came into play, I think there was a very striking difference between how you led The Table and how people that you 'answered to' led The Table. I think that should be made quite noteworthy.

I was at the final service and know what happened before

that and what happened after that. And I think that your style of leadership, and who you are, allowed the members of the church to process it in a certain way. There was no way to process it well but I think that they [members] had faith in how you would handle the situation that we were given. I will leave that as it is; However, I would not have participated in *Drag Me to the Pulpit* the same way under any other pastor. *(Dawn: I appreciate that.)* I don't think I would have been allowed to by any other pastor.

[One of the comments I get the most, particularly during my time pastoring The Table, is that I'm not really very 'pastory,' to which I always say, well, thank you, that's a high compliment. I appreciate that. So, Veronika, thank you.]

Is there something you learned or experienced during your time or your journey with The Table that helped your thinking and BE-ing?

(A reminder to readers: Veronika Electronika is a Drag Queen persona of a person named Steve. While Drag, to his own admission, is performative, I hope by now you have discerned that Steve's faith is not performative. Not in the least. Steve is a devout Christian man in his own right. Veronika Electronika is part of his ministry, a focused part in fact. One that creates a space for God to work through his creative abilities as a performer; and to be light in the darkness.)

That is such a big question. It is a very intimate relationship when in the pulpit and speaking to people. People 'lift the lid'[6] quite often when they are sitting and listening to the preacher. They really want to be able to absorb it, so they listen with a different set of ears sometimes. I have to respect that relationship. It is somewhat different when I am emceeing a show or

---

6. 'lift the lid,' i.e., open themselves up spiritually or engage with the vulnerability of their spirituality

event, or at a political rally, it is different. [In the pulpit] somebody is allowing you into a very intimate part of their being, you know, it is their soul, their spirit. They are not just listening with their ears and their mind, they are not being so analytical. You [a preacher] can really affect the person who is listening to you in profound ways, that you could not in a different room.

I think many legislators have discovered that. When a person starts preaching from a pulpit in a political atmosphere, I think it causes people to feel guilty, or feel bad, when they do not take what the speaker is saying to heart, because they are saying it in a *"preachy"* way. I think it is very dangerous because you can be a false prophet and you can be a false pastor. One can be prophesying, knowing what they are saying may not be true or beneficial to whomever is listening.

Many times it is what we are experiencing in State and Federal Legislatures around the country right now. I think that is a huge disservice to the Church[7], in general. It is such a gross way of trying to manipulate the population by *Christian guilt-shaming* them. [It operates as someone in high authority saying] We [legislators] are telling you to hate these people; we need to make legislation against them; and if you do not, then you are not one of us. People then think, *why am I feeling like this*? They do not realize it is because of the method of delivery and the words that the speaker is using. I will also say that I have always detested "pastor voice," where they use the dynamics of a voice. It is a manipulation and hypnotization tactic. It is why I have always really tried to be conversational when I am preaching.

For example, I got escorted out of a church service once because the pastor was incessantly nodding his head and, as I

---

7. *Church.* When the word "church" is capitalized it refers to the Institutional body, as in the highest polity of a particular faith or denomination; as in 'the wider church.' When "church" is used lowercase it refers to the local church. When Veronika says 'disservice to the Church' she refers to all churches, everywhere, generally speaking.

looked around, I realized the congregation began to nod theirs in time with his. I spoke up about it because he had literally hypnotized this church. What he said was blasphemous. It was terrible. Awful. It was totally anti-biblical. I could not stay still, so I stood up and called it out, right in front of him and everyone. Needless to say, I got kicked out of the church. But it was worth it because what he was doing was harming people and what he was saying was total bullshit. I think that we have witnessed that many times in many state legislatures around the country. And I think people are so caught up in the theatrics and theater of the Church; It is too easy to do because people really love theatre.

I recently had a revelation as I have been thinking about this: God and faith are way older than religion and I feel like people have lost that concept. Religious liberty, freedom of religion, freedom for religion and on and on. Religion has been the root of many of the world's plights. If you are a true Believer, you have to understand that faith has nothing to do with religion. God, creation, love and all that stuff has as little to do with religion. It is the same as a grocery store saying it contributes to your healthy body. No. It is a method of delivery.

Religion is a method of delivery (good and/or bad) of love and faith and godliness. People are *golden calf-ing* religions. They are giving religion way too much clout when that is not the point. People have a lot of faith in religion, instead of faith in God. Many times there are people in pulpits who preach [religion] because their bank accounts are attached to it. Religion has always been a bad delivery system for faith.

I feel like anytime I get the opportunity to really lean into my spiritual self, I learn more and more about things like that. Because I am asking [God]; and if you ask, you will get answers. Whether or not you give credit to those answers, that is up to you. That is part of your own journey. I wish people did that more often versus just letting [pastors] feed them. You are giving somebody way too much access to your soul when you just give them carte blanche. A true Rabbi, a true Pastor, a true Teacher would give you more respect and allow you to have wiggle room for your own faith instead of giving you rules and circumstances.

When I came I was ____ and when I left I was ____.

First, there are so many witty ways to answer this question. When you give the answers to these kinds of questions, I feel like you need to ask them to paint a portrait of their answers. Literally, like give them a stretched piece of canvas. As I answer this question, it is going to be [long pause]—

—In the margins I will say, I have not changed a whole lot in my life, as a whole. I still identify with the six-year-old me; I still identify with the sixteen year old me; And the thirty-six year old me. I still identify with all these versions of myself. However, I have experienced moments of change and metamorphosis. So I will say, when I came I was curious and when I left I was satisfied.

[I asked this clarifying question: Is that Steve or Veronika, or both?]

I will say that's Steve. When Veronika came she felt complimented; she felt appreciative. And when she left, she felt humbled.

I do not know how to contrast my two answers with each other because Veronika is not a real person. Veronika is a character. For Steve to be asked to do this, [preaching] in character, I was very appreciative. I thought it was super cool. In the end, I was humbled because I have lived through the experience. I think to myself... 'And especially if you raised a couple of eyebrows. More especially, if you raised Pastor Dawn's eyebrows.'

What is your greatest joy now?

Just the act of living through it and breaking through potential boundaries I felt I may have had either spiritually, scholastically or physically. I think my greatest joy is knowing that I can do it. I can be behind a pulpit, in heels or not, and still be effective; and still be able to stick it to the certain kind of person who says *you have no place in that spot. Or, that behind a pulpit is not some place you belong.* I feel like if you can do that successfully, it should not matter what you wear, it should not matter. Because in Christ there is no male, no female. There is no gender. There is no this or that. All of those arguments are moot. It just does not matter. Anytime you are able to manifest that in real life, you take away all the credibility for all the people who want to try and take credit for being so godly. I am a more satisfied person knowing that they are full of shit.

Is there any part of your story we did not talk about that you would like to share?

I want to make sure we address the title of the chapter, *Veronika's New Stage*. I want to make sure that we identify what *staging* is. I encounter new stages all the time. Being "on stage" behind a pulpit has unique properties to it. It allowed me to embrace the idea of being an entertainer, being an educator, being a friend, being susceptible to spirituality and questions. That is why that stage was new. As an entertainer, one is not often allowed all of those experiences when on stage. If I was asked, what was Veronika's new stage? Or what did the 'new stage' mean to you? I would say it was an opportunity to use the gifts I have been given in a new way, with a new audience, in a new space.

It has also allowed me to take what I learned from being on that 'new stage' and use it in other places. So it is a new method of delivery, not just a place. I have learned that I can use what I learned on that new stage in other areas of my life. I often remember those moments being behind the pulpit at The Table as something that I hope I get to experience similarly again. The fact that The Table [as an organization] no longer exists, does not negate the fact that I can use those experiences in other places.

In the end, for me, the *new stage* I encountered goes into my bag of tricks. I want to make sure that that becomes part of the story here. I want to make sure people get that. Ultimately, just because The Table is no longer, does not mean that that stage isn't still there. I think you can look at it in real world terms and say, you can take those experiences with you no matter where you are. And because this is a metaphysical stage and a spiritual stage, it cannot be taken from you. It cannot be removed. So, I ask people to search for *new stages* for themselves wherever they can find them.

What would you like to leave as a public witness for others who may read this?

Never underestimate your ability to change the world.

I have lots of side stories. I got in trouble in my freshman year of college. At the time I was very baby-Christian. I was never a Bible thumper or Jesus Freak or anything like that. However, I got in trouble once for writing an essay. We had to write a family dynamic story and I used God and Jesus in a father-son drama. I got in such trouble because I humanized the divine relationship between God and Jesus. And it was not even a Christian or religious school!

I wrote about struggles like, *'Dad, do I really have to go and do this? Like, can't you send somebody else? Can't someone else go? I have other things I want to do.'* It was a drama, yet, I got wrung through the wringer. I think because I wrote more than what they wanted. I went through creation, to the birth of Christ, to crucifixion, to rebirth of Christ in the dynamic of a family relationship. And I think to get to the answer of this question, *is there anything I want to leave as a public witness for others—* Even though you feel like you may be tasked with something that you may feel is impossible, or that you may not really want to do, or you do not quite understand what it is, but you know that there is good intention to it, embrace it as much as you can. Ask for help along the way. Jesus did all of those things.

Could Jesus have saved the world without his disciples? That is a huge question. The answer should be "yes" but if the answer is "yes," then why didn't He? Why did He need disciples? He knew that one of them was going to betray Him. It is a mind-blowing concept for the Savior of the world to need a bunch of other dudes to make it happen; Or chicks, or whoever it is. An all powerful God should have been able to do it themself. So we have to ask, what didn't work the first time? that God had to have the Son come to earth.

So what I would leave for people is, allow yourself the opportunity to know that you can ask questions, you can ask for help. You can do all of the things you feel like you can.

I hope one of the things readers get out of this book is that they can belong to a church home. They can have faith in a God who allows them to ask questions and to live through experiences; and that they should not be ashamed of asking questions. They should not be scared to be jarred a little bit.

I am hoping that as they read this they feel an ember burning inside and think, "I want to do that," or "I want to go to a church that does this," or "I want to experience that," or "I'm sorry that I did this, or I wish I hadn't done that." I am hoping this book can be that for them. Because a book like this is potentially going to be one of those that somebody [i.e. non-affirming person, homophobe, transphobe, xenophobe, conservative pastor, etc.] holds up and tries to say, 'look at this shit that they're trying to do.'

I am hoping that when somebody reads this, that they are able to see that journeys of faith are personal. And that even for pastors, your personal journey of faith is often shared with a group. But that is not to make your journey somebody else's journey; Rather, to allow others to validate their own.

Pastor's Afternote:
I always got fantastic feedback about the way in which Veronika was "a light in the darkness." That is what was said which incidentally, is straight from scripture. Whether or not the person who said it knew it I don't know—Truth be told, Veronika is a light-hearted being, talking about serious things.

The Drag Me to the Pulpit preaching series allowed me to engage with a very well-known Drag performer in our area, in a red state, as an answer to limitations that were put on the Drag and LGBTQ+ community that were also rooted in what our Governor considered religious protections and religious freedoms. I pastor with a very wide theological lens[8], we believe the Spirit moves at will. And that it is in the tripart God [Creator, Son and Holy Spirit] that we live and move and have our being. That [pastoral] authority and freedom specifically is what caused me to respond to the political legislative action banning Drag. My response to that was, well, if we are going to claim religious freedoms and religious exemptions, then I also am going to claim religious freedoms and religious exemption. I also am going to be, as scripture would say, a balm in the Gilead of this legislative process. Tennessee has passed more anti-lgbt and anti-trans laws than any state (at the time of this writing). We are known as the Slate of Hate, sadly. So my answer to that, my response to that as a public theologian and

---

8. For more information on what ELCA Lutherans believe visit https://www.elca.org/about/what-we-believe

as a pastor, was to find a way to bring strength and light into the pulpit. And Veronika, you were the way to make that happen.

I was so grateful to Veronika's advice for us to search for new stages for ourselves wherever we can find them. I began this book deliberately with the final sermon I delivered in my pulpit at The Table, during which I did my best to encourage all of us. A reminder that The Table may stop here but the story does not stop here. We can all take the seeds that were sown and find some new soil to plant them in and germinate them, along with God, and see what new things grow. This book is one of those new things that has grown out of the joy and the pain of having been part of The Table.

PART IV
COMMUNITY CONNECTIONS

Music City Sisters of Perpetual Indulgence
TDOR, IDOA, Transletes, and Prom
LifeNotes & Wondering Questions
At The Table God's Beloved Sheet Music

The Table was not only a place of worship, for some it was a home away from home—A safe place in the community at large that allowed folks/x to come together and laugh, get and give support, serve as allies to others, play games, eat, drink (non-alcoholic) and be merry. Community events at The Table were some of the few sober places queer folk could gather.

We were an advocacy and outreach ministry. Our bread was gluten free and we provided both wine and grape juice as standard because we had folks/x in recovery. Some churches have "gluten free options" but that was not enough for me. In the spirit of 'if one is not free, none are free,' it was more of a commitment to establish that we were gluten free. We tasked those of us without a sensitivity, to adjust (not the other way around, as is most often the case). Intention matters.

Game nights, social gatherings, dinners, and service projects were all sober spaces. Those of us without that challenge were tasked with adjusting. Again, not the other way around, as is most often the case. Drug and alcohol abuse are rampant in our community; Rampant because the internal struggle and external life challenges make living in our community more complex than our non-LGBTQ+ counterparts. Familial and societal rejection often cause us to think terrible thoughts, that sometimes lead to terrible decision making, that sometimes lead to abuses.

The Table did its best to meet people where they were, no judgement, only unconditional love. We aimed not to reinvent the wheel but rather provide community events and resources that were not otherwise being provided. We intentionally, as our Welcome Statement says, strived for whole person wellness. And we actively sought unity—not only with each other but also with ourselves. Sobriety was often the hinge pin in that journey.

There is no way to adequately describe all the many ways The Table filled the gaps. A few of the highlights are captured below and in the footnotes all throughout the book. We partnered with any non or for profit group who was "doing the work." That being, tending to the needs of the LGBTQ+ community with the caveat that their organization's mission met the mission and vision of ours.

Some of the other events we (or I) attended and participated in were the Invocation at Metro Nashville Council, plenary speaker, emcee Pride Spirituality Night (held during Pride Month), serve as Board Member on various community oversight boards or advocacy councils, student support, keynote addresses, protests on Legislative Plaza when sessions were discerning Bills and Laws (mainly anti-LGBT). I spoke at numerous civic events and provided words of prayer or public advocacy support. When our member, Olivia Hill was elected as Member at-Large, I was honored to speak at her Investiture Ceremony. Olivia, as you read, is the first transgender woman to be elected to office in the State of Tennessee. She currently serves constituents in the Greater Nashville area and is doing a remarkable job. What a joy to see her face, and others' in the room, brimming with pride and excitement. Not only for the history of being elected, but because as a native Nashvillian, we know that Olivia has a deep and abiding love for our city and those who reside here.

Suffice it to say, The Table was all over. We were in schools, stores, parks, churches, government buildings, hospitals, restaurants, advocacy groups, social gatherings…we served the needs of others and we did it with grit, grace, and gratitude. The Table was a very special place doing very special work.

MUSIC CITY SISTERS OF PERPETUAL INDULGENCE (MCSPI)

Fewer Community Partners have been as important and instrumental to the success of the ministry and advocacy work of The Table as the Music City Sisters. In earlier chapters their work was noted by several of us. They are a force to be reckoned with, to be sure. The history of the Sisters of Perpetual Indulgence[1] began in the 1970s during the AIDS Epidemic. The hard-hit area of San Francisco required action from brave souls who were not afraid of the disease nor of the people who suffered from it. As a societal ill, in my opinion, AIDS pales in comparison to the disease of racism, homophobia, transphobia and xenophobia. AIDS causes a severe loss of the body's cellular immunity greatly lowering the resistance to infection. The latter causes a rotting of the soul that infects the body and that of those in proximity, often causing resistance to the healing balm of unconditional love. For that reason, the Sisters and I became fast friends and remain so to this day.

I first learned of the Music City Sisters when I attended a spring prom dance at a local church in midtown. Turns out, 'The Sisters' were the financial underwriters of the event. Dressed in Drag (called manifesting) several Sisters were at the event to show their support of the youth and to have light-hearted conversation that worked to destigmatize all sorts of negative talk concerning LGBTQ+ life. I won't derail this conversation about the many lies and myths told about us, as they are readily available on the interwebs. I will focus on the good work of the Sisters, most especially in Nashville and the surrounding area.

---

1. To learn more visit https://en.wikipedia.org/wiki/Sisters_of_Perpetual_Indulgence. Many cities have their own Chapter and can be found by internet search. In Nashville, TN visit Music City Sisters at https://www.musiccitysisters.com/

The current Abbess is Sister Sawyer Ladybits who over the years has become a very dear friend. (Veronika Electronika, whom you read about earlier, is also a nun whose name is Sister Reya Sunshine.)

The Table began partnering with the Music City Sisters in 2019, even prior to our official launch. If there was a good deed to be done, in the name of promulgating joy and advocating for youth, we did it together. The success of our "spring prom" was so positive that in a few short years, we began hosting a "winter formal" in addition. The students loved it, the parents were grateful their (gay) kids had a safe space to celebrate. We provided food, music, and special entertainment by local artists, choreographed particularly in a family-friendly atmosphere. Together we created a safe space for LGBTQ+ youth to celebrate and be celebrated.

During our winter formal in 2023, I was taken by surprise when I was surrounded by Sister Sawyer Ladybits, Sister Helen Heels, Sister Terry Yaki, Sister Pursefonee Ophelia Bitz and Sister Freeda Plai, along with members of The Table, and youth at the dance. As it turns out, on occasion, the Sisters "bestow sainthood" upon *individuals who embody their mission and values of universal joy, community service, and expiation of stigmatic guilt.* It was my night to receive such an honor. I was to become known as "Saint Dusk to Dawn." Never in my life have I been held in such love and honor by a group of drag queen nuns. Well, except at my ordination, when they manifested in full habit and sat among the other ordained pastors in attendance.

The Music City Sisters will forever hold a candle of light and joy glowing in my heart. On behalf of our city and queer community, thank you, each one of you, for your service of love and compassion for all of us.

TDOR, IDOA, TRANSLETES, AND PROM

Transgender Day of Remembrance & Resilience (TDOR)

Transgender Day of Remembrance & Resilience[1], November 20th, is the annual day of mourning for transgender people who have died by violence or suicide brought about by racism, transphobia, religious discrimination, and family rejection. At The Table we dedicated our worship service closest to this annual day of recognition. It is a solemn day as names are read in full (names chosen by the individual with their proper pronouns accordingly), we light candles, sing songs, read scripture and hear from guest preachers and speakers of transgender experience.

I believe every human has two God-given rights: a life well lived and a death well lived. My chaplain self is very comfortable with the experience of death, I find it to be sacred, warm and inviting. In the queer community, many deaths are experienced in violent ways. That violence works to detract from the holy and sacred life God gave to that individual.

We did our best to honor them by calling their age, location, chosen name and pronouns. Sometimes, this is the only recognition of their full identity at a service of their remembrance. We honored them because their lives mattered.

Intersex Day of Awareness (IDOA)

October 26th is the day set aside to raise awareness for our Intersex Community. Similar to how and why TDOR came about, Intersex Day of Awareness elevates and honors the lived

---

1. TDOR. We typically retrieved names from this database. Use with caution. https://tdor.translivesmatter.info/

experience of intersex people. As a bi+ person, I can attest that "erasure" is real. Erasure refers to the habit of those without the lived experience to deny its existence or validity.[2]

Intersex folks face discrimination in ways that many of us in the LGBTQA community do not or cannot relate to. At the time of their birth many intersex people have decisions made for them while they are infants. For those who do not, challenges may come later in life when discoveries are made during otherwise regularly scheduled medical care and testing.

IDOA exists to address the stigma and discrimination against intersex people while creating space for them to speak and be seen. Just as we dedicated a Sunday service in November to TDOR, we also dedicated a Sunday service in October to IDOA. Speakers from the community and special music was provided.

Transletes & Prom

The Table was not a family congregation, per se. Quite by happenstance we were all adults 18+. That is not to say kids and parents were not welcome, it is more that adults are who attended. To close that gap in service to all, we were active in community advocacy events. Two events became our focus: a bi-annual dance for LGBTQ+ high schoolers and a community-wide sporting event we called *Transletes* (it has since changed names for safety reasons).

---

2. I am choosing to use an example from my experience so as not to further injure our intersex siblings. Regarding "erasure:" For instance, what I hear often is some version of 'can't you just pick a side?' Also, the ignorance of folks who would rather assume than read a book say things like, 'oh, being bi+ must be fun, you get to have twice the sex.' The reality of intersex life is real, not conjured up. Intersex babies often undergo surgery to "correct" their body. Parents of infants are told they are doing the right and responsible thing. It is not always true. A later discovery often causes psychological damage and an attempted erasure of the now adult person's lived experience. Intersex Day of Awareness aims to give back a portion of identity that was taken in infancy.

Governor Bill Lee and many other state leaders have diligently worked to legislate hate, hate mongering and discrimination against LGBQ+ folks. And Transgender people, more specifically. In 2021, Gov. Bill Lee began signing laws banning transgender students from playing sports in their schools. Annually, Governor Lee has continued to sign discriminatory bills of this nature, some requiring the state to pull funding from public schools that allow transgender students. Lee has also signed bills prohibiting private schools the same.

In an effort to be a balm, I often used my public leverage as a faith leader to create opportunities for families to experience similar activities their non-LGBTQ+ counterparts did.

I previously mentioned our partnership with MCSPI for the bi-annual dance. For *Transletes* we partnered with Nashville Pride and PFLAG Nashville, along with a few other smaller grassroots organizations. Kickball was the sport of the day. All children were invited to play with many adults playing and coaching as well. *Transletes* was a specific creation to clap back at the passing of the Transgender Athlete Bill here in TN (SB0228).

LIFENOTES & WONDERING QUESTIONS

LifeNotes developed from my preaching and was an answer to the reality that one can have music without worship but cannot have worship without music. When we began, I had no means of making music as that is a skill and gift God left out of the recipe when making me. (Thank goodness for Wesley!) I mentioned how challenging it was to find life giving lessons in scripture sometimes because of the bombastic nature of story and phraseology. Words and language matter. In the queer community, I cannot emphasize this enough.

Following exegesis and writing, I commonly experienced the need for loud music, thrashing cymbals, pounding drums, along with flowing streams, soft lyrics and dancing rhythms. This led me to long walks and drives to gander at God's beauty in nature. That, paired with my large and diverse library of music, led me to create *LifeNotes*. Simply put, meditative questions ("wondering question") paired with a secular song.

The point being, as I stated in my chapter, humans have created the separation lines between what is sacred and what is secular. My belief is that if God is the creator of all that is, everything is sacred in some way, shape, or form. Thus, if we channel our thoughts and curiosity in a spiritual way, applying that discernment and presence of prayer and gratitude, we can listen to any genre of music and find a way to pray through it. We process a host of thoughts and feelings dubbed 'the human experience'. We also traipse through what is often referred to [in spiritual terms] as 'the dark night of the soul.'[1]

In the early months of gathering in person, I began to inte-

---

1. In modernity, the "dark night of the soul" is used to describe a crisis of faith or a difficult, painful period or experience in our life. Formally, "The Dark Night of the Soul" is a poem written by St. John of the Cross, circa 1577.

grate listening to a "reflection song." Nine times out of ten it was a non-religious song and most often an acoustic version of whatever it was. Yes, though you may not be aware, there is a gift certain musicians have that allows them to transform even the hardest of hardcore into either easy listening or a gentle, stripped down acoustic version. This is what I would have used as a reflection song.

In a way that is both foreign and familiar, we are drawn closer to the bosom of God and to the center of our soul by pairing familiar lyrics with a tune our mind already knows. That was the *reframe* and *reform* theological aspects of the music. What became the *reclaim* was the addition of a "wondering question." The question followed scripture and the theme of the sermon, providing a simple meditative opportunity similar to Lectio Divina. I invited folks to consider how God could be at work in their life, [either previously or currently] through the text, the sermon, the music and the lyrics.

This brought together the Word of God, the wonder of God and the sovereignty of God, something queer folks have often had to struggle with. We crossed genres. We crossed boundaries. We crossed lines of division. We found our wholeness one note, one lyric, one prayer at a time. Below is a sampling of the songs and wondering questions we used during worship:

- *Crazy Train,* (yes, Ozzy). How is Jesus concerned with our mental health and wellness as it relates to the struggles of life? How do we take care of one another?
- *You've Got a Friend.* How does David's struggles relate to your life? Does God comfort you as God comforted David?
- *RESPECT,* (yes, Aretha) Consider the ways God is present in your relationships and healthy boundaries with yourself and others.

- *Shake It Off,* (of course we are Swifties!). How do you cope when others treat you in hurtful ways? How do you reclaim your belovedness in your relationship with Jesus?
- *Photograph.* When you have lost important people or relationships, do you allow God to comfort you? How do you let go or hold on?
- *Say Something.* Allow your pain to surface, then reclaim your strength. You are here because you are resilient.
- *Born This Way,* (our gal Gaga!). How do you understand your belovedness as a sacred being?
- *Way Over Yonder.* Heaven is all around you, not "up there." How can you live your life in the present moment (and day!) claiming God's blessings on your life, right here, right now?
- *Beautiful,* (Aguilera). Don't let anyone say you are worthless. God uniquely designed your life to see the world through your eyes. You are beloved.

The *LifeNotes* tribute would not be complete without sharing the hymn we wrote together with Wesley. The only proper and lifegiving way for me to end this section is to invite you to read the lyrics below. If you are a person of LGBTQ+ experience, let them wash over you and bring you a delicate peace. If you are a person of non-LGBTQ+ experience, allow the words to transform your thoughts so that they may grow within you a deeper sense of why these words matter to us; why it is so critically important to have people like you in our corner, and why I, personally, am so grateful you have dedicated your time to reading this book.

AT THE TABLE GOD'S BELOVED SHEET MUSIC

Bennett, Cheux, King, Siatos

BEACH SPRING
8.7.8.7 D

Used with permission.[1]

---

1. Bennett, D., Cheux, K., King, W., Siatos, L. "At The Table, God's Beloved." Unpublished Manuscript. 2025. Used with permission.

PART V
THE MAKING AND BREAKING OF A PASTOR

"I distinctly remember talking to God and saying, 'I don't know what they need.' God answered, 'Ask them.' I said, 'I'm not sure how to help them.' Again, God whispered to me, 'Ask them.'"

When it came time to write my chapter and discern its placement, last was the only fitting place. When I preside at Communion, I serve the people first, the Assistant Minister next, and I am served last. To me, that makes the most sense. To me it is what is meant by Servant Leadership. If you feed them, they will come. If you serve them, they will heal. If you practice humility, God will be honored. It is the only way any of this ministry business makes any amount of sensible sense to me. Why God called me, I still do not fully understand. All I know for sure is that, next to my children, it is my most sacred gift.

At the start of my first ministry call, I wrote my ordination oath on my office wall in large letters with a permanent marker. It reads:

> *Dawn, care for God's people, bear their burdens,*
> *and do not betray their confidence.*
> *So discipline yourself in life and teaching*
> *that you preserve the truth,*
> *giving no occasion for false security*
> *or illusory hope.*
> *Witness faithfully in Word and deed to all people.*
> *Give and receive comfort*
> *as you serve within the Church.*
> *And, be of good courage, for God has called you,*
> *and your labor in the Lord is not in vain.*

Never did I think, not one moment, that telling the story of the life, death and resurrection of The Table would be as necessary and healing as it has become. Not only for the people, but also for me. It is an honor to serve the spiritual needs of others. Bearing another's burdens is a complex matrix of balance, to be sure.

When our security was literally ripped out from underneath us, it seemed there was no hope. As we scattered—some in hiding, some in depression, some in dismay, some in fear—over time we found each other in the spiritual realm and were able to piece together an honorable and honest, yet often painful, peek inside a ministry that, for the ELCA and for the LGBTQ+ community, was quite an anomaly.

Some things can never be made entirely whole again. So to facilitate our spiritual healing, and in an effort to restore [some] balance, most folks participated in this writing project by interview while others found it cathartic to write out their story. As I said to the guest writers, and I will say to you, dear reader, sometimes in life we have to create our own closure and our own joy. By God's grace, the writing of these chapters hopefully helped us on our way.

With so much I could easily contribute to the book in terms of my experience, I am choosing to answer the same questions the others have, acknowledging it is but a morsel. During this project, most especially the interviews, I found that I too had experiences that were in keeping and in response to either the ways in which I provided ministry, or the ways in which I was the recipient thereof. One thing is for certain, The Table has left an indelible impression on my life, and I will be forever thankful for the honor and privilege of having been its pastor.

There will never be another ministry like The Table. Those of us who collectively built it, shared its joys and sorrows, and who have taken our seeds with us are surely blessed beyond measure that it existed at all. Baruch Hashem Adonai.[1]

How did you find The Table and how did you find Pastor Dawn?

In 1997 I was called to serve in ministry. My children were all young, two of them toddlers. My then spouse was not keen on the idea of being a pastor's spouse so I had to defer what would come next in that service. My Dad, who was still alive at the time, gave me what was likely the most important piece of advice I have received in my adult life. He said, "Dawn Marie, do not ever underestimate the truth that raising a family is ministry." For the next twenty years I dedicated my time, talent and treasure to the flock in front of me.

I worked part-time and full-time along the way; completed a variety of educational degrees and certifications in a few fields (mostly helping professions); built a few companies and shifted from employee to employer and back to employee. There were

---

1. One of my tattoos; In Hebrew, "Blessed be the Name of the Lord."

many changes and experiences along the way that continued to prick my spirit and challenge my thoughts.

It is no mystery, and I have previously shared publicly, that I come from a big family with many siblings, and most of us are gay. I use "gay" because it's easier for me in conversation. If it really matters to you, I am a cisgender, pan/bisexual female. I love hearts, not parts. I have a son and other relatives who balance their lives between the endpoints of the SOGI scale[2]. Me and my sibs were raised in the Catholic tradition and my children were raised in the ELCA Lutheran tradition. Neither Church was particularly kind to gay folks. Thankfully the ELCA experienced a fracture in 2009, allowing non-affirming, conservative folks an opportunity to find a sheepfold more in line with their conservative values. I digress.

I recall, as a child, plenty of my friends coming to (Catholic) church with me. When it came time for Communion I had to whisper, "I'll be right back." It never sat well with me and I always felt like Jesus would be bummed out that my friend was left out of the meal. That is likely where all this began for me. As I grew, I watched as one by one my gay siblings came out and were either kicked out or to the curb. That added to my pain of seeing people I love mistreated in the name of God.

I transitioned to the ELCA Lutheran church while married and found a home there. Over time I experienced a divorce and as my kids grew, one came out and later transitioned. Although, by now, the Church would have been a kind place for us all, divorce left us a fractured family. So much so, that we still have not fully recovered from it all these many years later. Even so, I continued off and on, in and out of non-denominational spaces and Lutheran spaces.

---

2. SOGI Scale refers to data we use to understand the diversity of lived experiences so as to improve healthcare, and inform policies related to LGBTQ+ individuals. Also see prior footnote on page 33.

Almost twenty years after my first spiritual awakening toward pastoral leadership, I knew I was again being called into ordained ministry. My Dad was still alive so I went and talked to him once more. You can guess how the conversation went because you are now reading this story.

Living in the Deep South has grown more and more difficult for me and my kids. Politically it is a terribly negative environment. No one has to look very far to find hate speech, biblical bastardizing or religious zealots ready to burn someone at the stake for being gay. Thankfully, we have a robust LGBTQ+ community here and while we may, at times, have to operate in covert fashion [because it can be literally physically risky and dangerous] we are a loving, supportive, strong group of queer folk and allies.

When I quit my corporate job to go to seminary, I was definitely older than most students and by far one of the only students who already knew why I was there, from day one. I had a clear sense of what God was calling me to do, which was to create space for gay folks to exist and participate in the Church in life-giving ways, whatever that meant for them. A bit of a plot twist occurred when I myself came face-to-face with my own sexuality that I kept under wraps my whole adult life. It became true that after all these years, I finally reached a place of safety— A place where I too could blossom into my full self and live my life more authentically.

During seminary my Dad died. He was my biggest champion and supporter in my ministry work. I also lost my partner, and my Academic Advisor. I could not understand how God would allow this. The grief, pain, constant ache and righteous anger were, at times, almost unbearable. From the bird's eye view, I began seminary with a strong support system on all sides and I finished on bloody stumps. But God. I credit my finishing to the young people who were around me at the time, who filled me with vim and vigor, who pushed, pulled and dragged me from semester to semester, as I waded through grief, loss, change and exegetical work. I credit my siblings who called, sent cards, sent money, came to visit, fed me and gave me a place to hide out from time to time. I credit my kids for calling and visiting more than just when they needed something. I credit and give thanks for the host of angelic friends, church folk and clergy colleagues who buoyed me during those years. Then, the day came. Graduation, and ultimately ordination.

I was ordained to the Ministry of Word and Sacrament on January 12, 2020 by The Rev. Dr. Kevin Strickland, Bishop of the Southeastern Synod, ELCA Lutheran Church. Despite the ups and downs of our several-year ministry-friendship-colleague relationship, I am grateful for his participation because without it The Table would not have launched. Yes, the plans were laid years before with my emeritus bishop. But by 2020, a signature on the dotted line is what was needed by my current bishop.

What neither of us knew at the time was that we were weeks away from a global pandemic. When that struck, like every pastor all over the world, I too had to pivot. I began preaching from my living room Sunday evenings, and the rest as they say is history— And you have read a great deal of it from others whose chapters have gone before me.

What was the condition of your faith prior to joining The Table?

My parents introduced me to Jesus when I was a little girl. I have never not known about Jesus but it was not until my early teens that I developed a personal relationship with Him. My sister is nine years my elder so I had a bedroom to myself and I believe that is where it really began for me. I went to church with my family. My Dad was a Deacon in the Catholic church so I was always there. (You read about some of it in the *Charis: Two PK's in a Pod* chapter.) Even though the Catholic church was not kind to my siblings, I never believed they (or me) were unworthy of anything. I always blamed that unkindness on the priests and the doctrine, not God. People can be mean and God gets blamed. A lot.

My faith has never been rooted in anyone but me and God. So in that respect, my faith was solid. I had plenty of church hurt though. That has a lot to do with why I am the kind of pastor I am. It is true, I am not very "pastory." I think what people mean is that I am unique and quite outside the lines of orthodoxy. They would be correct. I am not a fan of organized religion, really. It has done a great deal of harm to both God and people. Religion is made by people and I think in our best intentions, we mean for it to be a healing program. I think we mean for it to be nurturing and edifying. Unfortunately, for nearly all of us, in the name of religion, many pastors, doctrines and religious authorities have shaved off our corners in an attempt to make us fit in their god-shaped hole. The trouble with that, for me, is that it may not be God's hole. And therein lies both the rub and the opportunity.

How would you describe your growth journey during your time with The Table?

Everything changed almost immediately. Well, for the church anyway. I had four years worth of church planting plans. We were to launch as a Dinner Church. Enter COVID-19. In all honesty, it was the best thing that could have happened to me and to us, at least in terms of church growth. I am a skilled Mission Development Pastor. Building and bringing to fruition previous companies, administration, and management were all skills I brought with me into ministry. I had a long history of public speaking way before preaching. I brought that too.

The biggest challenge in the beginning was that there were no people, no building and no programming before the pandemic hit—we are literally talking weeks. So, I began by networking, calling and emailing mostly LGBTQ+ organizations, to find out who they were, what they did and if The Table (or me) could be helpful to them in any way. My first community partners were the Music City Sisters of Perpetual Indulgence, PFLAG Nashville, Nashville Pride, and (now) Tennessee Pride Chamber. I made quick friends with as many gay clergy in the area as I could find. (There aren't many, but we do exist. And no, we don't glow in the dark.)

I began to reach out locally and nationally to give interviews and talk about the ministry. I quickly learned we were more unique than I realized. Not only that, there would be much more blowback than I anticipated, socially and politically. Thankfully, I come from a large New England family, most of us are gay, I had two blue collar entrepreneurial parents who taught me well, a supportive Bishop and local clergy support to help coach and guide me. We took off like a rocket. Praise God from whom all blessings flow...

I experienced early that my children and family would need to somehow be protected from the negative and nasty news, articles, and heathenistic claims that were already being made about me. I had some serious but tender conversations with them: do not read the comments; they are not talking about your mother; no, I won't tell you the details; and yes, I have a therapist and a safety plan. This [safety plan] would become very necessary over the years and I learned a great deal more about non-violent communication, self-defense, nuancing public commentary and how to use the spiritual Armor of God to protect my mind and my embodied faith life.

With the advice of clergy colleagues who are older, wiser and more experienced than me, I began to develop a Dawn life and a Pastor Dawn life. Rarely the two shall meet. Pastoring a church like The Table, filled with heaps of celebration, trauma, drama, pain and joy like non-gay folks do not know, I created patterns for myself and boundaries that I could live within. Many people would ask me, 'how do you do it and keep your head?' I would say, 'I come off the grid, I tell no one, and I make no apologies.' Now you know why there were times you could not get ahold of me or I did not answer your email. I was likely off-grid for health and wellness reasons. Every so often I post a status on my socials: "Closed for Spiritual Maintenance." Like I said, no apologies.

I went to the beach twice a year (I began that in seminary, actually) as self-care. Growing up on an island and living in landlocked Tennessee often created, for me, what felt like a clog in the emotional drain of life. I had to get to the water. Specifically the sunset. I still go there. It is my happy place, where I meet with God; where I find my wholeness.

I would say the greatest growth I experienced over the years is learning how to pastor a group of people, who were not my relatives, in a way that allowed them to know I have love for them, without becoming enmeshed in their personal lives. For a place like The Table, we were more than a "church," as you have read in these chapters, we were a family. Yes, I was the pastor. Yes, I had responsibilities over and against those who were members. Still, we were family. Queer life requires "chosen family." Some communities do not understand what this means, but if you are part of the LGBTQ+ community, you know full well.

Describe the lifecycle of the 3 R's in your faith journey.

The 3 R's developed naturally out of my exegesis[3]. Each week I found myself scouring scripture and some days I would be so angry by the end of my study. I often found myself saying,

---

3. *Exegesis* is defined as critical explanation or interpretation of a text, especially of scripture. It is how pastors prepare to preach.

Lord I cannot bring these people this fucking message! It is not life-giving. It is not helpful. And they are bleeding out as it is already, so we have to find a way to turn it around. That was the humble beginnings of the 3 R's pedagogy. Without bastardizing scripture, and without proof texting, or taking things out of context, I began reading a little extra here and there, more than the lectionary text, sometimes the entire chapter; coupled with a host of commentaries.

By my own decision I was a lectionary preacher. Mainline Catholicism and Protestantism follow a 3-year text cycle. My decision to follow the same lection was deliberate, because the LGBTQ+ community is constantly experiencing a barrage of religious discrimination. And the vast majority is due to the aforementioned stumblings during exegesis. I thought all right, well then, we are going to use the same weekly readings that every other church uses. We (God and me) are going to mine for life-giving messages that are directly impacting the queer community. That way no matter what Catholic or Protestant church a person went to in the morning [if they went elsewhere] they would hear a message at our service on that same scripture. When folks came to worship Sunday night at The Table, the message was very different. It centered the *lived experiences* of the *queer* community.

Sermonizing began to form naturally. So much of scripture is so bombastic. And it is so vulgar and so violent. Frankly, pastoring a queer church, there is enough vulgarity and enough violence already just in that lived experience that we did not need any more, especially from God [or religious dogma considering itself a god]. When overlaying scripture onto a people group who have been bludgeoned with the Bible on numerous occasions, sometimes finding life-giving messaging can really be quite a quest. Sometimes there just does not seem to be anything good in there. If there is one thing I remember saying the most it was "lean in, lean in"—We lean in until we find ourselves located in the text and then seek to find how we can bring some life out of it.

I would ask myself and God, how can we [me and God] *reframe* this so it is not so death dealing? And how can we *reform* our thoughts so that we are not stuck in the quagmire of our upbringing? How can we *reform* some new thoughts around this piece of scripture, which ultimately lead to action steps (*reclaiming*) that will help us develop life giving behaviors so that we are not so self-incriminating. If God is not incriminating us for who we are and how we are wired, why are we doing it to ourselves? As Veronika mentioned in her chapter, it is all about the delivery.

The 3 R's is a solid practice. Even still, it is hard work to retrain our brain. We first have to work on unwiring. Only then can we begin rewiring. It is a lot of work and it can be exhausting work. Yet, it became a way of life at The Table. So much so that in every sermon I gave for the last several years, each of the concepts were worked into the sermon somewhere. I am a practical and liberation theologian. My personal belief is you have to use what you learn or it is both meaningless and powerless.

In reviewing my sermon approach and exegesis, I noticed a pattern forming. In the world of preaching, the most respectful and impactful way to preach is to the people in front of you. That means it is the duty of the preacher to change with the context, not make the context change for us. For me that meant speaking to an lgbtq-centric church. To give you an idea of the expanse of that challenge, our folks were lesbian, gay, bisexual, asexual, intersex, transgender, cisgender, gender nonbinary, gender fluid, neurodivergent, black, white, latinx, some were gay parents, some had gay kids, some had different learning styles, some had disabilities (mental and physical), and some were allies. Some were active or recovering alcoholics, some recovering or active drug addicts. Some were recovering

Catholics, some recovering Baptists; some were nones and some were dones. Some Atheist, Agnostic, Pagan and affirming Protestants. Some were Exvangelicals, some Pentecostal. Needless to say, there was no "typical" member.

Back to the weekly sermonizing task. What began to happen, particularly when using Bible commentaries, I found it necessary to use all kinds of translations not just the NRSV which is the standard go to in Protestant churches. Because it was an LGBTQ-centric church and because the Church is the primary offender, having caused the breach in the health and wellness of LGBTQ people—most especially where faith and spiritual wellness is concerned—the Church needs to be the one to repair the breach. As the pastor and the preacher, I absorbed the responsibility to do what I could to repair the breach.

That, over time, morphed into teaching people how to think differently about scripture; and helping people by giving them more options about how to think (*reframing*). They naturally began to develop a new theology in their own worldview. They then began to develop new choices about behavior (*reforming*). Before long, folks began to *reclaim* a new healthy faith life. It was an amazing process to watch. (Not much in this world is amazing. Lasagna and movies are not amazing. Seeing God in nature, watching a life transformed and revived, that is amazing.)

I was preaching and ministering to folks who (some) had been thrown out of their childhood or previous church. Some literally, like with physical hands on their bodies [which is to this day unfathomable to me]. Some were abused physically and sexually by their pastor or parent or guardian. All of us were told by somebody that being gay was wrong and sinful. If not by family, at work. If not there, then on the tv screen or in the voting booth. To be clear, Tennessee (and many other states) is a right-to-work state. That means we can be fired, evicted, refused treatment and services, and legally discriminated against for the sole reason of being gay. Paint that with a God brush and you can begin to get an inkling of the ministry The Table took on.

Over the period of five years, we moved worship space four times. Each time we moved, we left the space better than we found it. Each time we moved, we inched closer to what most "churches" consider sacred space. Don't be fooled by this, Beloveds, every space is sacred space in queer life. We renovated each space we were in. It represented our lived experience as gay folks and we were proud to call it our own. Our last worship space we named *Open Seating Chapel*; it was the most beautiful cathedral-like stone chapel. It had stained glass windows and floor to ceiling sashes in Progressive Pride flag colors. Our paraments were rainbow, our prayer tree was a fern we hung prayers on, like ornaments. We called our service *Open Seating: Good Food for Hungry Folks*. We displayed our Mission Statement proudly in the sanctuary along with affirming artwork commissioned especially for us. It was a holy, sacred, wonderful space to be together.

How did Pastor Dawn's leadership style differ from what you were used to or experienced with?

I know my leadership style is outside the box. No one has or had to tell me that. My entire life has been outside the box, to be honest. So when it comes to pastoring, I pastor the way I live my life: authentically, compassionately, and practically. We were a bunch of queer people, some of us Christians, some recovering Christians, all of us practicing what it could possibly mean to love others, when not all of us loved ourselves; and love God, when we were told God absolutely finds us disgusting and abominable. Try that on for size.

What approach would you have taken? The one that occurred and appealed to me is to ask two questions, and only two: *What do you need?* and *How can I help you?* That was my style. If what I did, or was about to do, or thought about doing, or made plans to do did not align with those two questions, I scrapped it and began anew.

Sometimes I began anew right smack dab in the middle of what was happening because that is what was required in the moment[4]—either to meet someone where they were, or to be in a position to be able to be of help. It required lots of listening, lots of waiting and more grace than I had sometimes (so I borrowed from God's storehouses). I admit, many of my colleagues did not understand. Oftentimes my Bishop did not understand. And definitely, his staff absolutely did not get it. To Wesley's earlier point, I decided that was okay, they did not need to get it, I did. And I did.

And then there was the ice cream. Everyone knew about my love for ice cream (it makes the world a better place!). Since we met at night, the folks developed a pastime of going to 5th & Broad after worship. They included me. One of my favorite things about Sundays grew to be going out for ice cream after worship—because it was cool. As the pastor, to be included in the ice cream runs, it made me feel like I was one of the gang. So it is a very high compliment to me that my leadership style is approachable. That is what being invited on the ice cream runs signaled to me. And that is my goal in life, to remain approachable. I do not want to be judgmental, I want to understand. And in order to do that, I have to remain approachable. That is my philosophy, anyway. It works well for me; it lets people know I care, for sure.

Call me weird, I have been called that most of my life. Call me looney, I am probably a bit off my rocker. Call me what you want. The people of The Table called me Dawn, Pastor Dawn, Pastor and PD. They knew the voice of their shepherd and I

---

4. This is the distinction of providing trauma-informed pastoral care (TiPC). For more information revisit Footnote 1, pg 26.

knew the voice of my sheep. And we worked very, very diligently at learning to recognize, understand, and value the voice of God among us. That is what matters.

How would you describe your growth journey during your time with The Table?

I distinctly remember feeling so small when I began preaching. Now, to be transparent, I had had decades of public speaking, workshop facilitation, business ownership, presentations and all that under my belt before I stepped into the pulpit. While in Divinity School I even won the Florence Conwell Prize for Preaching. What a surprise that was! But I have to tell you, the overwhelming responsibility of knowing that my words carry weight, oooff. There were days God and I duked it out, for sure! So many times I said, "You want me to say what?! Outloud?! No way. I can't." All this while knowing deep within me that preaching is one of my spiritual gifts. Each time I was met in my quiet time with *groanings too deep for words* (Romans 8:26-27). God always won, naturally. So, was there something in particular I experienced? Yes, the intimate knowledge that if ever I feel totally comfortable in the pulpit, it is time to leave it.

I trust God completely. Ministry at The Table was no joke. Yes, we laughed. A lot. But ministry was serious business. We were a bunch of gays ministering to a bunch of gays. Nothing says hilariously serious like that dynamic. There were so many highlights I cannot begin to name them. Every chapter in this book describes a front row seat I was privileged to have, absolutely. Some others were the articles and interviews I was part of. It gave me a platform to talk about the amazing work we were doing. People all around the country were so impressed that we were a church and were so dedicated to providing a place of healing—and in the Deep South! That is what was such a different twist.

I suppose though, if I had to name one growth in particular that helped my thinking and being, it would be how important the responsibility of *languaging*[5] is. To language something is to wrap words around it, to support its meaning, to prove its point, or to make it understandable. In preaching and advocacy work, most especially within the convolution of theology, religious discrimination and LGBTQ+ life, word choice is a critical intersection. Proverbs 18:21 reads, "Death and life are in the power of the tongue, and those who love it and indulge it will eat its fruit and bear the consequences of their words."[6] Likewise, James 3:1 reads, "Not many of you should become teachers, my fellow believers, because you know that we who teach will be judged more strictly."[7] The rest of James 3 focuses on the power of the tongue, comparing it to a small fire that can cause great damage.

So, *languaging* is the most important, meaningful, difficult, rewarding, and intimate experience I had during my time pastoring The Table.

When I came I was _____ and when I left I was _____.

When I came I was determined to lead people to discover a new freedom in their faith. When I left I was sure God would help me find a way to make beauty from the ashes.

---

5. "*Languaging*" refers to the active, dynamic process of using language to create meaning, build understanding, and shape our experiences and interactions. It is not just about speaking or writing, but rather the broader, ongoing process of using language to think, learn, and interact with the world. This includes considering how language choices shape our perceptions, influence social interactions, and contribute to the construction of identity. As one might surmise, paint this responsibility with a "God brush" and it becomes exponential. This is precisely why I am a trauma-informed pastor and provide this training as often as I can to others.

6. The Holy Bible: The Amplified Bible. 1987. 2015. La Habra, CA: The Lockman Foundation.

7. Holy Bible, New International Version. 1973, 1978, 1984, 2011. Biblica, Inc. Used by permission. All rights reserved worldwide.

What is your greatest joy now?

Part of my greatest joy is that this project came to life. I had an opportunity to write about my experience pastoring The Table in 2024. However, I was in the middle of completing a chaplain residency at the hospital and I did not have the bandwidth to write. As disappointed as I was to turn down the opportunity [because never in my wildest dreams did I think it would come back around], I am so thankful I did decline. Had I written the story in 2024, it would be a continuation of the many interviews and articles I participated in up to that point.

Now, I can honestly say, my joy in this project far exceeds anything I could have imagined. Now I can honestly say, the project pays homage to the beautiful lives that have been touched, to the hard work, emotional exhaustion, mental gymnastics, celebrations, tears, fears, and mountains that were climbed by the people who so graciously and generously shared their stories in these pages.

By far, my greatest joy, second only to my children, is having been given the honor and privilege of pastoring this church. The experience has changed my life drastically. I learned so much and gained so much; it is quite immeasurable, I believe. I trust that joy in my ministry will continue but it would not be nearly as rich as it is without my experiences at The Table.

Is there any part of your story that we did not talk about that you would like to share?

At the time of the sudden, unexpected and emotionally brutal closing of the ministry, rumors immediately began to fly. For the record, the Bishop addressed the congregation to say that I was/am in "good standing" and that I have done nothing wrong. This is absolutely true. My good standing is evidenced by the reality that I am under a new ministry call in a nearby city. Still, rumors flew and I was unable to address them—as in not permitted. I was bound by an MOU (Memorandum of Understanding), essentially an NDA only in church speak, because supposedly that makes it okay? better? somehow more palatable?—Nonetheless, for my own security on many sides, I remained silent.

To maintain my own integrity and security, I will continue to abide by the MOU while at the same time, do what I can to demystify the closing and following few months. I was never given the exact reason for closing but what I was given was less than a week to completely shut down a vibrant five-year ministry. In their respective chapters, a few folks made a statement regarding their attendance at the final worship service and their interpretation of things. I agree with Veronika, there *"was no way to process it well but I think that they [members] had faith in how [I] would handle the situation that we were given."*

I took myself off the grid for a few months after the closure; it was a matter of survival and self-care for me. I have had to explain to some folks about the tragedy of my experience. Because there was Dawn's experience, then there was Pastor Dawn's experience. It did not make my grief process any more or any less than the other members and community partners, but it was very *different.* When we closed, and most especially as abruptly and emotionally violent as it was, I lost my church and I lost my only means of income. Yes, I lost my church but I also lost my flock, the congregation whom I took an oath to shepherd and care for. During the interview with Veronika, she jumped in, *"I'm going to correct you. You did not lose it. It was taken from you. Let's be clear about that. That's different."* Yes, thank you, that is different, yes. And you know what else was taken from me—my church family.

My personal church family was taken from me, so I had nowhere to take my grief. I could not take it to my church family, where the members got to. They got to talk and be together. *(Veronika again: In my opinion, that happened because of rules and regulations of the institutional organization, not because you wanted it that way. But because you were not allowed to.)* It was hard because I had never experienced such Church-inflicted pain. I had never experienced Church-inflicted anguish before then. But sadly, we became very intimately acquainted.

I was in a terrible depression, I lost a lot of weight, and was alone without colleagues, church friends, or family. Some may say I could talk to them if I chose to. Not true. First, I had an MOU that kept me silenced, even when I had no factual information. Second, my clergy colleagues all had questions that I was not allowed to answer. It was difficult for them also because their own church members had questions and rumors which could not be answered, either. Emails, phone calls, text messages, DMs from all around the country flooded my inboxes. It was so incredibly overwhelming. So, I took myself off the grid.

There were only two people who could get through to me, and my therapist. Everyone else was either blocked or sent to voicemail. I did not even tell my family the whole truth (which sounds a bit funny since I didn't and still don't even know the whole truth. I digress). If you know me personally, you also know most of my family has been rejected by our Catholic upbringing and the Church. So, no, I could not bear to hear any version of, 'well, yes Dawn, that's why we don't "do" church.' No thank you, it was already painful enough. To this day my public narrative is, "we lost our funding." It will remain that way.

What I am able and willing to share is the update I gave to my local Deanery[8] a few months after the closure, when I was able to scrape myself together enough to be in public. Keep in mind, they had not seen me or heard from me in about three months. They had questions [that I could not answer, and have

---

8. A Deanery is our local ELCA Lutheran clergy group.

not to this day] but they were compassionate enough to not ask and instead greeted me with kindness and love. I am ever so grateful for compassionate friends and colleagues. And I must say, thank you again, Matt, for holding my hand through it. Here is the statement I read to them, that I now share with you:

> *It's so good to be back in community with you. I'm sure many of you are wondering about the status of The Table and may still be confused about a letter that was circulated through the Deanery in early October.*
>
> *While I am unable to talk about a Synod office meeting I had on October 7th, I am happy to share with you that on October 6th I returned to the pulpit after a much-needed September sabbatical. Worship was fantastic; After which we stayed for fellowship and discussions about incoming Advisory Team members. We also discussed our Fall planning meeting slated for October 18th, to capture the flourishing and blossoming of the ministry.*
>
> *As [the bishop] shared, while very sudden and quite unexpected, we held our final worship service Sunday, October 13th. Bishop stayed after to talk to the community and made the announcement that it was decided to put the ministry on what he called "permanent pause."*
>
> *The Table was a vibrant community with fantastic lay leadership and several volunteer outreach ministries. We were also financially able to support the physical needs of several folks in our LGBTQ+ community. It was my joy and privilege to serve as Mission Development pastor for the past five years and I look forward to seeing what new things grow from its seeds.*
>
> *In November I made the decision to go on leave from call as I discern my next steps—and I appreciate your support and*

collegiality during this season. Many of you have reached out with prayers of concern. I am very grateful for that and ask that you continue to keep me and our former congregation in prayer as many of us are still processing grief and hardship.
In the meantime, I have been blessed to provide pulpit supply at [local churches] and look forward to continuing to help out where I can.

When I was a kid I learned a phrase, 'do you want to be bitter or better?' Well, it is true what they say, church hurt is [by far] the worst hurt. At the same time, I trust and believe that God who is all-knowing and compassionate, while crying right along with me [and the others] also was in the background working on our next set of steps. What you are reading, at least in my opinion, is a good set of next steps. We are all better for The Table's existence. In every way.

What would you like to leave as a public witness for others who may read this?

Faith is not a cookie cutter experience. Religion might try to be a group effort but faith is an individual growth process. I am not a religious person, I am a faithful person. At the many stops along my faith formation road, I have learned religion will confuse you, beliefs will betray you, but faith will never fail you. What does it mean to have faith? Simply put, it is to have belief, trust and hope in something. For me, that is a divine Life Force greater than myself.

I have journeyed far and wide with God (who I call *Abba*, but not as in Daddy, Father, etc., despite its translation, but as in my *Absolute Best Buddy Always*). I have been confused by many religious teachings and dogmas, I am sure you have too. I have definitely betrayed myself and had others betray me: my confidences, my best interests, my trust and my love. I have never in all my half-century plus years of living been failed by my belief in myself or my Abba. There have been many times where it has been just the two of us rolling through life. I am sure you have likely been there too.

I believe one of the greatest travesties is to draw lines of division. What is often meant for good purposes, in our human greed and bent toward a me-and-mine outlook, lines separate more than they unite. If the Creator made everything on earth and in heaven then lines between sacred and secular is folly. They are not God's lines. They are not the Spirit's lines. They are human's lines. We made those lines. And so, I believe it is up to us to blur them, or to erase them altogether.

What I believe with every fiber of my being is that when we look into the eyes of another person or living thing, we are looking squarely into the reflection of God. Most especially and importantly, with regard to looking into each other's eyes with intimacy (into-me-you-see), we often discover that we have unique access into the life and worldview of that person. It is quite a privilege [and responsibility] to behold. If there is an action step I leave for you Beloveds, I invite you to slow down and take this knowledge and awareness deep inside your heart and conscience. Because I also believe with every fiber of my being that our greatest challenge in this life is to be good stewards of that privilege.

After the outpouring of each chapter, I am not sure there is much more to say. Except maybe, thank you. Thank you for reading this far. Thank you for your curiosity, your prayers, any tears you may have shed on our behalf or those of someone you love. What I would say moving forward, is to, as best you can, believe in yourself. Trust that you are fearfully, uniquely and wonderfully made. There is no other you than you. Have faith in yourself because God had enough faith in you and God's self to create you oh so long ago (Jeremiah 1:5).

I will close with the words I gave as a Benediction at the end of every worship service:

I invite you to stand with me now as we pray our Sending Prayer. We pray this prayer outloud together because we believe that when we speak these words over ourselves, outloud, that God hears our words and takes them deep into the center of God's bosom. They are stirred up and shaken up and given back to us in the form of a renewed faith. So I invite you [and you also, dear reader] *to pray with me now:*

> *We are a blessing. We are not a burden.*
> *The world is a kinder and more wonderful place*
>   *because we are in it.*
> *We are loved by God*
>   *and cherished for who we are in our Creator's eyes.*
> *We go with confidence knowing*
>   *we are a unique and precious creation. Amen.*

Beloveds, I love you, God loves you, and don't let anyone tell you different! Be well.

This may be the end of the book but, by God's grace, it is not the end of the story.

May it be so.
Amen.

www.ingramcontent.com/pod-product-compliance
Lightning Source LLC
LaVergne TN
LVHW012042070526
838202LV00056B/5570